Ghost Stories from the Ghosts' Point of View
Trilogy Vol. 2

Tina Erwin, CDR USN (Ret)

Ghost Stories from the Ghosts' Point of View Trilogy Vol. 2

Tina Erwin, CDR USN (Ret)

Ghost Stories from the Ghosts' Point of View,
Trilogy Vol. 2

Copyright © 2019 Tina Erwin
Third Edition Published 2022
Second Edition Published 2016
First Publication 2014

Published by Tina Erwin

ISBN-13: 978-1-7322673-0-5

Cover Photography by Tina Erwin
Cover Location: Botanical Gardens,
Rio de Janeiro, Brazil

Works by Tina Erwin

The Lightworker's Guide to Healing Grief

The Lightworker's Guide to Everyday Karma

Ghost Stories from the Ghosts' Point of View, Trilogy, Vol. 1

Ghost Stories from the Ghosts' Point of View, Trilogy, Vol. 2

Ghost Stories from the Ghosts' Point of View, Trilogy, Vol. 3

Soul Evolution, Past Lives and Karmic Ties

Karma and Frequency

The Crossing Over Prayer Book

Special Notice to the Reader:

WARNING
Due to the mature nature of the content of this book, which may deal with tragic and/or violent death, reader discretion is advised. These true stories are intended for mature audiences only.

Acknowledgments

Tremendous effort is required to put forth the information you are about to read, and no successful author accomplishes anything alone. I am blessed to have wonderful people supporting me as I share this critical knowledge of how the living can help the dead.

My loyal and loving husband has earned my undying gratitude for supporting all of my psychic efforts and for his conscientious editing work on these books.

I would like to gratefully acknowledge the support and critical assistance of my entire publishing team: my daughter, Jeanne Marie Erwin Coronado, my daughters–in-law Amee Erwin, and Monica Lane. A special thanks to my sister Andrea, and her daughter Marisa Harris for all the efforts to help the dead in all the locations we have visited over the years. Also, a very special thank you to Marisa for the house she spent helping me to format this book!

Thanks to all of your dedication, hard work

and attention to detail, the world will get to know the true stories of those ghostly souls who will now live in our hearts forever.

Dedication

This entire book series is dedicated to all of my friends who, over the years, have taught me so much.

This dedication is also intended for all of those brave souls who asked for help in assisting many a ghostly soul to cross over.

And finally, I am deeply grateful for the Spiritual Beings who unfailingly assist us all to guide lost and lonely souls to the Heaven World.

Preface

"I love your stories, but you know, they're all so sad! Sometimes they're really hard to read." A. E.

Virtually all of my very true stories seem to have a rather sad element. Yes, they do, that is the point. Ghosts need help crossing over, finding the peace and love that only the Heaven World can provide. No matter how much you love and miss the person in your life who has died, you can never provide them with the hope and healing that they will receive in the Heaven World.

The point of these stories has never been to illicit sadness in my readers. The goal of these ghostly experiences is to open people's hearts to the need for compassion for those who have died. Wishing and hoping that a loved one, friend, or past soul somehow found the light is merely that: wishing and hoping. These stories are opening the door to the cold reality of what it is like to be dead and desperately need the help of the living to cross over.

I would guess that roughly 2% of souls

actually cross over into the Heaven World on their own. Based on my experience of helping millions of souls, yes, millions of souls to cross over, the truth is that I would estimate most souls never actually make it to that crossing over point. These people languish in the dismal dimensions of the sooty nether world. They all need help, especially children and anyone who died a violent, depressed, or fearful death.

I wish with all my heart that these statistics were different or at least reversed, but they are not. No one knows what to do at death. Let us help them.

I would like to point out that 100% of these stories have a happy ending, which is the final embrace of the light and the precious escort by the Angels of Transition.

Looks like I gave the endings away! But then this is the final ending we all want for ourselves, and those we love.

I hope you will enjoy these stories and learn to see ghosts in a new light so that you will want to help them all.

Tina Erwin, CDR USN [Ret.]

Testimonials

"This is a fantastic and gripping set of stories! It is definitely something that everyone needs to ponder about life and death. It's a continuum of experience that you so dramatically illustrate through the stories in Ghost Stories from the Ghosts' Point of View Volumes 1 and 2. I was amazed and awestruck how the ghosts, people we don't even know, can impact us and what the resolution looks like from the ghosts' point of view and also for the human who had the experience with the ghosts. What an amazing and impactful book!"

Suzanne Strisower, Author, Life Purpose Expert & Spiritual Life Coach at www.AwakenToYourLifePurpose.com

"I hosted a paranormal radio show on the Internet for five years and I had Tina Erwin as a guest on my show several times. I found her to be a very compassionate and knowledgeable person about spirits trapped in that in-between world of the living and the dead. Tina is very skillful in assisting spirits in moving on to the next phase after they have left their human body. It was very comforting to talk to her about my mother who had died of cancer. I knew that my mother had successfully crossed over, but Tina explained to me that our loved ones who have crossed over can connect with us in our dreams from the other side. I have seen my mother make brief appearances in my dreams several times since then and I am always happy to see her. Also, Tina assisted my girlfriend in helping an active spirit cross over to the other side. We no longer hear footsteps in the night, nor experience lights that click off by themselves. I greatly appreciated her work!"

Ron Mills, former host of The Chosen on Talktainmentradio.com

"My friend, Kevin and I went out at 2 am one night in early summer in July 2014. Kevin has been obsessed with WW II and Nazi bunkers for a long time. We went to a specific bunker that night carrying artifacts with us which came from several other bunkers. We buried them in the ground while the moon was shining on us. While we did this, we recited The Crossing Over Prayer (that Tina Erwin wrote) to help transition all those souls who lost their lives at that place about 70 Earth years ago during World War II.

After we buried the artifacts in the ground and covered them with soil, we did The Crossing Over Prayer again 4 times. We faced all 4 directions around the bunker. As we were doing this, we both felt a release and a gratefulness coming from the souls we helped to go to the Heavenly realm. There was a warm night breeze when we went back home. Our hearts where full of grace."

Maarten Horst is the Host and Founder of "ET-First Contact Radio" in Holland and has done over 500 interviews with people disclosing their encounters with Spirit and ET's, including Tina Erwin.

"When my Mother passed, she was supposed to die within 30 minutes when they disconnected everything in ICU. She did not die for 26 hours; I prayed the crossing over prayer for days. 4 days after she died, in the middle of the night, I woke to a bright light that filled my bedroom. There is no doubt in my mind that that was when my Mother crossed over, there was such peace and true understanding that she had successfully crossed over."

Chris D. San Diego, CA

"I have relied upon The Crossing Over Prayer innumerable times! Peace and calm always follow. I am grateful that I have been provided the tools to make a difference. Thank you. [SEP]Love and gratitude always."

Becky H. Virginia Beach, VA

"Thank you so much for sharing your prayer. I went to Harlem to visit my grandmother and because so many bad things happened in that apartment in the projects, I think I brought something really dark back with me. Back home in Vermont I found myself feeling heavy, slow, and stuck. I saw orbs and other strange things. My vision felt blurry. I saw things out of the corner of my eye, mostly around my face. The final straw came when I woke up because I heard a crash in my living room. I got out of bed lit a candle and recited that Crossing Over Prayer a few times. My living room felt so dark to me, and I did not want to spend time there. Now I want to spend time in my living room. Thank you, thank you!"

Diana P., Vermont

"On three different occasions I have contacted Tina for help and guidance in assisting souls to ascend onto a higher realm. During this process The Crossing Over Prayer is used. Letting loved ones go after death is so difficult when we want to hold on but, in essence, we are giving them the best gift possible, and it provides a closure that could

otherwise take years to achieve. I have also used the "Prayer for My Beloved Animal" a number of times, especially this past spring when I lost my cat, Shadow, who had been in my life for 21 years. I'm very thankful to have knowledge of these prayers, and the understanding that we have the power to assist Angels with the souls that may require help ascending."

Cindy S. Virginia Beach, VA

"Our client was selling his home and the sale was falling apart for the third time. The client's wife had passed away and we asked permission from the client to read The Crossing Over Prayer because it was the only thing we could think of to do at the time. We read the prayer and the house sale closed in less than a week!"

Jeanette, Realtor, San Diego, CA

"Avoid a few speed bumps along the way to the hereafter with this book. Listen to what Tina Erwin has to say about ghosts and what their reality is really like. This book is full of fascinating stories, along with great information and insight."

Wendy Garrett, Conscious Living Radio

Foreword

As the former host of a CBS radio show called "Hot Leads Cold Cases" for many years, I have had the opportunity to interview some of the most fascinating leaders in the world on such topics as parapsychology, ufology, psychic detective work, mediumship, neuroscience, astrophysics, psychology, medical intuition, remote viewing, astrobiology, corporate and military spy programs, and much more.

Occasionally, there is a guest who just sticks out in your mind. You remember your conversation with them for years afterward. Tina Erwin is one of these people. I interviewed her several times on my show. She was smart, analytic, cool-headed and was able to access profound levels of intuitive wisdom. As a retired Naval Commander who worked for the submarine force in the U.S. Navy, she was clearly used to performing functions that involved taking charge of others, assuming enormous responsibility, giving orders, operating within a larger group, fearlessly confronting the unknown, and managing the needs of both men and women in stressful situations.

Although she didn't share this with many people, she was also utilizing her highly tuned intuitive skills at the same time. When she later became a psychic medium, healer and paranormal investigator, Tina began to step into her own higher powers. She has used these skills to help people in many ways. Tina is able to help grieving relatives of dead family members by explaining life after death, as well as helping people whose homes are haunted by ghosts by accessing different periods in time to coax these human spirits toward the Divine light.

For somebody like me, an attorney who became a trained psychic detective, medium, remote viewer and medical intuitive, I have an especially strong appreciation for people like Tina who have managed to travel across worlds that normally don't collide.

Tina came onto my show one night and we talked about the first book in her trilogy series "Ghost Stories from the Ghosts' Point of View, Trilogy, Vol. 1." The interview was going quite well, and we had a perfect Skype connection. We talked about spirits, the way she locates them in distant homes by virtue of her clairvoyant techniques, how she listens to their stories, often of violent or sudden deaths, their reasons for lingering on earth after their death, and her efforts to steer them toward the Divine light and God.

After about forty-five minutes, I decided to ask her a very important question about her technique in steering lost souls toward the Divine light. I wanted to know why and how lost souls needed to be given food and blankets. After all, without a physical body, how can a ghost be either hungry or tired? Well, all hell broke loose! Immediately after I posed the question, the Skype line went crazy with unusual static. It was impossible to hear each other. My CBS producer had to interrupt the show and call Tina back on a different line. She and I understood instantly that it was the result of spirit interference in our interview. The spirits clearly wanted Tina to keep some information about how she handles lost souls confidential. I never forgot that show.

Her trilogy, "Ghost Stories from the Ghosts' Point of View," is an unusual series when it comes to paranormal and ghost hunting tales because, as the title suggests, Tina writes about her dialogues with ghosts and lost spirits. Most mediums can channel the words of spirits, which are often cryptic and confusing, not to mention extremely difficult to remember once out of trance mode. Most paranormal investigators can locate the presence of spirits and recognize their activities at a location. Tina's method is very unusual for several reasons.

First, Tina does a significant portion of her work at a distance and not on location. That means when she is doing a typical house cleansing or trying to identify the causes of a haunting, she is often doing the work remotely. She doesn't actually enter the home or building.

Second, she not only identifies the various spirits – which often exist within different time zones on top of the same location, something Tina calls "stacks" of time – but she engages in extensive conversations with them. She talks to the ghosts about their problems, whether they know they are dead, the reasons why they have chosen to stay earth-bound, and describes their clothing, their precious objects, homes, family, and historical background in tremendous precise detail.

Third, Tina transcribes her ghostly conversations using the various dialects and accents of the ghosts – such as their Scottish brogue or African slave broken English. The reader begins to feel like they are right there alongside Tina and the ghost in a different slice of time.

Because Tina has a military background and an excellent recollection of American history, she easily slips into an elegant historical account for each of her ghost's individual stories. Her book is a beautiful tribute to the spirits most people can't see or have long since forgotten. Tina's efforts to heal these broken and lost souls by helping them find the Divine light will undoubtedly be her most important legacy during her own lifetime.

Nancy du Tertre
"The Skeptical Psychic"
www.theskepticalpsychic.com

Table of Contents

Mission Statement

The purpose of this book is to offer you a different view of what it is like to leave your body at death.

The hope of this book is that you will cease your fear of souls who have left their physical bodies and begin to understand their situation.

The opportunity of this book is the opening of your compassionate heart to those who need help crossing over.

Send them your prayers.

Send these souls your love.

Request Angels of Transition as you say The Crossing Over Prayer to assist them in crossing into the light, no matter their method of death, no matter what this person may have been like in life, and no matter whether or not you loved them or even knew them.

Service to the dead is one of the most compassionate and important acts of kindness, a living person can ever do.

No ghost is at peace until he or she finally crosses over into the light. Your service to

Ghost Stories from the Ghosts' Point of View
them means the difference between
continual feelings of fear and abandonment,
cold and pain versus the joy, and the hopeful
delight of crossing into heaven.

What is that Haunting Feeling?

Everyone loves a good ghost story. The endless fascination with ghost stories goes back centuries. All traditions talk about 'ancestors,' some in reverential tones and some in the genre of fear. We readily embrace the concept that there is something utterly unknown about ghosts, why they haunt us, what their story is and how we fit into the mix. Why do we love to be scared by the unknown? Perhaps a more important observation is that we love how we feel when we explore the stories of the dead and/or we have a 'close encounter' with a ghost.

But what are we really feeling when we are in the presence of a ghost? What is that haunting feeling? Being haunted means that you are in the presence of a 4th dimensional being. Think about it, the person who is occupying the space next to you is not in the same dimension, is not physically alive in the way you think that someone is 'alive,' but you can feel each other's presence just the same. This person may still think she is alive even though she may have died 320 years ago.

You can feel each other's presence some of the time. The dead moving in their 4th dimensional world often have no idea you are standing there at all. And we chronically preoccupied humans meandering throughout the 3rd dimension mostly don't know that a ghost is standing next to us either. However, there are those unique situations where the two dimensions collide.

When we moved into our house in San Diego in 1988, my family would randomly smell someone smoking a pipe in the room that was my office. In another section of the house, we would notice that memorably acrid wafting of a just-lit birthday candle – not just any candle, but the distinct smell of birthday candles. These smells were always in the exact same places in the house. The odoriferous aromas appeared at seemingly random times. It felt as if someone used that back room as a den and the area in our front hall was a dining room where birthdays were celebrated.

But we were the second owners of the house, so there was no dining room in our front hall and the back room was now an office. The previous owners had no one who smoked a pipe. Before those owners, the area had not had any previous buildings. This was (amazingly) the first dwelling on this piece of property, so we weren't dealing with a house from a previous time.

It became creepier, because we often felt as if we could see someone out of the corners of our eye. There was the unnerving sense that we were not alone in the house. There was that fleeting feeling of something more being in the house with us, and that odd sense continually nagged at all of us.

I knew that we had a ghost and over a period of time I learned how to see the dead through a process called remote viewing. Remote viewing is a psychic skill, which means that the intuitive person is able to see into the ether and determine who or what is affecting the living.

The first time I remote viewed our home I realized that it was haunted. It was haunted by souls who could 'see' me and assumed that because they could see and sense me, that I could help them. Several of them simply followed me home. It was unnerving to remove them that first time. I had five souls waiting to cross over. Back then, that seemed to be a terrifying number of ghosts, but how few do you have to have for it to seem manageable?

We did finally resolve that incongruous pipe, and the birthday candle smell. One of our first recognizable hauntings was a man who committed suicide and who had indeed smoked a pipe. Another was a child, hoping for one more birthday cake with those pretty, special candles. And then they kept coming.

They arrived so frequently that eventually the ghostly fear, thrill, weirdness, and uniqueness began to completely wear thin and we were left with that feeling of "Sigh, another ghost, okay, lets help them out." When you do this long enough it's not scary anymore, it's work. The glamour was gone.

Ghost Stories from the Ghosts' Point of View
What Is It Like to See, Sense or Feel a Ghost?

The collision of the 3rd and 4th dimensions means that someone realizes that a ghost is present. The ghost may or may not know that he or she has died and may or may not realize that they are actually making their presence known to living people. I believe that, on a certain level, this is a bit creepy for the dead as well. There are many ways that people, who do not consider themselves intuitive on any level, can 'see a ghost.'

Seeing a ghost can mean that you actually observe a filmy, foggy white substance appear in front of you, or notice something wafting down a hallway. They can also appear as an orb or fog in a photograph.

You may 'see a ghost' appear to you in what is termed 'full aspect.' In this case, the ghost looks like a living person. If you saw this soul, you would swear that he or she was still alive. There are stories all over the world of people kindly stopping for hitchhikers on dark and stormy nights, having a conversation with this person and then when the conversation lulls, looking over to find that they are speaking to eerily, creepy thin air. Yes, that's when you definitely have chills. This is when the questions come flying into your head: how can this happen? What did just happen? Should you even believe what you think you saw? But this couldn't possibly be true, but yet, you know it was true. How do you sort this out within yourself???

It can become even more incomprehensible if you and a ghost are occupying the same space, at the exact same moment, but you are separated by possibly hundreds of years of time. This is a difficult concept to wrap your brain around, but it is important to embrace it. Can two objects occupy the same space? The answer is yes, if they are separated by time and dimension. This concept directly applies to ghosts. Let's look at a specific example.

Once, the middle-school aged daughter of a friend of mine was at the grocery store walking down the baking aisle when she walked right through a ghost. She didn't realize it at the time. The sensation was so powerful for her that she was excited to tell her mom when she got home, that something had happened in the grocery store. When she related the experience, she said that she walked through air that felt like she was walking through water – she felt chilled briefly and then it was over. Then she returned to shopping for brownies.

It is pretty disturbing on a certain level. When her mom related the story, she asked me what could have happened. I told her that I suspected it was one of the many drunks that occupy grocery stores. Yes, lots of grocery stores are haunted because they make such a big deal out of their alcohol counters. Any location that sells alcohol will be haunted. My friend listened to her daughter, but after she talked to me, she elected not explain what really happened to her. How do you explain this to someone who is twelve?

You sense the presence of a ghost because there is the part of you that can see the ghost. You cannot consciously describe what your subconscious can see, but you know in that inner part of you that knows things, that there is a soul near you.

You see something fleeting out of the corner of your eye.

A door closes by itself: it may not be the wind or an air current, but rather a ghost trying to get your attention.

You hear words but not audibly, and only in certain places.

A dream lingers in the threadbare reaches of your mind, where you see a person who you know has died. This person may share a message, beg for help, or seem to let you know of his or her presence. If the dream continues, and the ghost lingers in a longing manner, something else is taking place. You will need to go deep within yourself to try to figure it out. Sometimes, the person is asking you for help in crossing over. How fortunate for you if you are reading this book, that you can use The Crossing Over Prayer© to help him or her to find the Heaven World.

Say the prayer at least three times. If you no longer have that dream, if you feel a sense of an almost imperceptible 'shift,' then you will know on that indefinable level, that you have performed a wonderful spiritual service. This will mean that the ghost has found the bliss of the Heaven World. The time has come to accept this as a reality of living in a mortal world, which can be influenced by the 4th dimensional world of the dead.

The Challenge for the Psychic: Changing the Paradigm

If you have any level of psychic ability, you may find that you occasionally know when a ghost is present.

Others know it and feel burdened by it. Some psychics are quite annoyed constantly knowing a ghost is present. Many psychics have no intention of helping the dead.

Then there is the psychic who tries to communicate with the dead person and gets fragmented bits and pieces of information thinking he or she can help the living. Mortal souls may need assistance with a troubling ghost, but the truth is that when you help the ghost, you automatically help the mortal person who can sense or see that ghost. If the psychic can do that, if he or she can move on that ghost, then both the living and the dead will find a sense of peace.

Finally, there are those seemingly intrepid 'ghost hunters' who keep looking for ghosts and then, when they find one, announce that they were scared to death that they found a ghost. Really? Why were you seeking them in the first place? Was it merely for the momentary thrill of being scared by what you cannot see?

This behavior is baffling, since ghosts are not that hard to find, just walk into any hospital, bar, or funeral parlor. Did you ever wonder why these hunters of the dead never look in these screamingly obvious places?

So let us change this psychic concept. If you are intuitive and you are reading this, or you do not think of yourself as psychic and you have a courageous and giving heart, then step up to the plate, change your thought paradigm and help the dead! Say The Crossing Over Prayer© at the end of this book at least three times, the most wonderful and helpful tool any psychic or ghost hunter can have for sending ghosts to the Heaven World.

If you want more specific prayers for a suicide or murder situation, the death of a child or a death by a wide variety of means, use The Crossing Over Prayer Book©. This is a marvelous tool book for anyone of any faith to use. Even if you 'don't have a particular faith,' there will be helpful prayers for you.

Pirates!

History is often flat and boring because it appears one dimensionally on a black and white page. Would it not be astounding to have a time machine so that you could visit the past and see firsthand what life held for our intrepid ancestors in the solid, comforting reality of three dimensions? This is why when you remote view a location, you slip like a bit of fog into the tiny crevices of someone's life. Initially, you become just slightly more than the proverbial 'fly on the wall.' However, within moments, your presence is visible to the people, the ghosts, who still think that they are living in that time. They have no idea that life and death have slipped past dictionary definitions and have entered the realm of science fiction. But for the dead and the psychic, what they are each seeing is real to them, in that moment of time. This skill of remote viewing offers the psychic a limited glimpse of the past, in real time.

'Real Time.' What does that mean? It

means that you, the psychic person, are a cosmic projection tenuously present in another time and space in the reality of that past currently existing time.

But life in real time is seldom as glamorous or exciting as a story or even boring history books make it seem. As you slide back, life in any sliver of time can be starkly terrifying for those ghostly people who keep living it over and over. Life everlasting can also be the 'everlasting' element that is the tortuous moment of your unrecognized death.

This particular remote view took me back to the fragile beginnings of our country, a time when the success of living day to day was never a guarantee and simply arriving here safely from Europe was a gamble. The events of this flash of time were anything but romantic, cavalier, or dashing.

Our ancestors, men, women, and children endured crushing hardships that make any written description automatically inadequate. Death, that great equalizer, ends our knowledge of a person's life. We all assume that souls magically move into heaven. Think about it, what else can people believe other than the dead of tragedies past must have moved on, that they must have gotten n past that final trauma that left them outside of the realm of the living?

But all too many of them have not moved

on, have not found anyone to help them, have not found that bridge to the light.

They have not found this light bridge because most of them have no idea that they died. The ordeal of their death was instantly rejected, because here, in the 4th dimension, logic can be so readily denied. But then really, how do you know you are dead?

That Creepy Feeling

Sometimes a dream is not merely a dream, is not simply a nighttime excursion into a nonsensical world. Sometimes a dream is a message from someone who needs help but may not fully understand just how much assistance he or she may need.

Sometimes a dream is a message from a ghost and if you are sensitive enough and perhaps compassionate enough to recognize the connection between what seems like a dream but feels totally different, you can help someone by showing them tremendous compassion. And this was the beginning of a fascinating connection to the past through the portal of a seemingly innocuous dream that came to my friend Colleen.

"Hi Tina, I called because I had a dream two nights ago that I wanted to talk to you about. In this dream I was drowning. I was screaming for someone to help me. When I awoke, I was exhausted; almost as if I had relived some terrible event that took place, but I don't know exactly when. I think what unnerved me is how real it felt, as if I was actually living something terrible. I don't seem to remember any details, just that the sense of drowning, of being cold and wet was overwhelming. I don't remember any more of the dream. But since then, I've had a tough time breathing, as if I can't quite get my breath. Oh, and my stomach feels funny, all crawly sort of. Do you think there's a connection between my dream and how I'm feeling?"

"Anything's possible. Usually when you have a dream that is that real, there is more to it than you may realize. Have you had any trouble breathing before this dream?"

"No, I've been fine. Everything's been pretty normal, ordinary. I thought I'd feel more relaxed since our mini vacation to the Outer Banks of North Carolina last week where I was vacationing with my family. It's so beautiful there. I feel this special kinship to that area and I'm not sure why. I loved walking the beach and I felt great while I was there but, I don't know, since I got back to Virginia, I don't feel like myself, and then this dream. Is it possible there's some type of connection?"

"I don't know, and I won't know anything else for sure until I take a look. So, let's go over what you've felt: trouble breathing, a crawly feeling in your stomach and a dream that you were drowning. Anything else?"

"I forgot to mention that I have had this dull persistent headache. Not quite a headache, you know, but a distracting ache that I can't get rid of no matter what I do. Oh, and I feel more tired than usual. Usually I'm full of energy, ready to take on the day, but since we returned from the beach, I'm simply not myself. Can you please check it out and see what you think?"

"Sure, I'll get back to you."

A Battle to the Death

I had suspected that Colleen had picked up a ghost or two on her Outer Banks trip. A generously sensitive person, she has always had an affinity for ghosts. When she can feel them so frequently, it is emotionally draining.

As I pondered her trip to the Outer Banks of North Carolina, I considered the thousands of ships that have perished there over the last 500 years. There has to be a reason they call this area of the Atlantic Ocean, the Graveyard of the Atlantic. Odds are pretty good that there is a ghost or two walking that windy, blustery beach. As I pondered this situation, I had no idea the depth and dimension this ghostly encounter would entail. But then again, there is no way to prepare yourself for what awaits you as you transition between time, space, and dimension. As I started this unusual journey into the past by remote viewing my friend and her home in Virginia, I realized that someone was waiting for me. I had no idea that a ghost in Virginia would take me to a completely different location in North Carolina.

Frankly, I cannot tell you exactly who was waiting for me. I could only identify that I detected a vague presence. The presence fluctuated from initially seeming to be male to definitely being female. I struggled with this for a while, and then gave up trying to sort it out. I sensed that someone wanted me to 'follow' him or her to a very different location, a place where souls needed help. Then this presence vanished. I began to understand how Dickens must have felt trying to create a description of the three vapory beings escorting Scrooge through The Christmas Carol: those eerie diaphanous guides you that you cannot fully see, but you can completely sense.

I took a deep breath and allowed the scene before me to slowly materialize into reality. Moving back in time, feeling oriented and allowing the present to melt away allows me to adjust to standing at a heartbreaking moment in history.

As the spiritual mist cleared, instantly I

could clearly see two ships engaged in a tremendous battle off what appeared to be the coast of North Carolina. I felt as if I was hovering above them, a detached, helpless observer. Both ships appeared to be endlessly stuck in time, somewhere around the late 1600s.

As I felt myself being drawn closer to the scene, I recognized with a sickening realization that this was not the expected violence of a classic Naval battle, but an appalling civilian massacre. Sometimes the anger, the rage and the incredulity of a given situation seem to be reflected by the intensity of the surrounding weather. The violence of the deluge infinitely complicated matters. This could have been a hurricane, judging by the intensity and height level of the black threatening, roiling, and unrelenting seas. There was streak lightning, crackling thunder, and staggering foamy green waves at least 30 - 40 feet high that seemed to be bludgeoning a floundering English galleon on all sides. The horror of the storm would surely have been bad enough but to have this entire event happening at night, with the endless lightning strikes illuminating the sharp reality of their perilous situation was heartrending. I dared not imagine what life was like on that vessel for anyone aboard. What I did not realize was that I was soon to receive an inside look.

Instantly, I was transported to the three-masted English galleon. There was the once proud English flag. This emblem of a great nation was tired, soaked, shredded and sagging, precariously attached to the top of the mast of the ship. Men, women, and children were screaming, crying, and struggling under the punishing sea storm, as their doomed ship denied them stable footing and any shelter from the unrelenting torment of the Atlantic Ocean weather.

This would have been horrible enough but as I watched, it suddenly went from perilous to disastrous.

I was transported onto the deck of this ill-fated ship. I began to feel the sheer intensity of their combined panic. Now I was able to hear and see firsthand the incredulous sense of horror as these men, women and children were subjected to relentless cannon blasts that were coming at them from all sides. There did not appear to be any way out. I steeled myself for what I inevitably knew I would witness: there would be no way for any of them to escape the icy, salt-watery fate that awaited them all.

"For God's sake, help us!"

The soul who suddenly began yelling, begging me to help, must have been a beautiful young woman. She was dressed in a partly shredded heavy, deep green, wool floor length dress. She was drenched to the skin; water seemed to be bubbling out of her mouth as she struggled to scream. There was a terrible gash on her head, the blood endlessly streaming into her drenched and matted, flaming red hair.

"Look! Help us! We're going to drown! The pirates are after us and the captain has lowered the sails! We can't escape! The water is coming in all around us. Can't you do something? Can't you help us? We don't want to die like this!"

The worst part was that she had no understanding that this fight was long ago lost. She kept reliving those terribly, tortuous, tragic moments just before and after her death, over and over and over.

The scattered screams in English and Irish accents, of what must have been several hundred terrified people, pierced my emotionally protective cloak of detached compassion. My heart went out to them.

"Help us! Please someone, God, please help us, we're drowning we're drowning! The pirates are after us!"

These are the screams of the eternally dying, the souls in denial, the souls already living in the house of yesterday, because tomorrow will never come for them.

As I surveyed the scene, the logistics of the situation became readily apparent. A pirate ship with masts at full billowing sail was blasting the English ship mercilessly. How the pirate ship was able to maneuver in this churning storm was baffling to me. It is impossible to pilot a full-masted ship in a heavy gale-force wind and rainstorm because of the danger of snapping those masts. Even if those masts survive, the sails themselves begin to shred in the severity of the storm.

Obviously, the English captain was trying to save his ship, so he brought the sails down. Once he did that, he was a sitting duck for the pirates who did not lower their sails. The risk the pirate captain ran was that to have the sails up meant that their ship could easily snap a mast, yet somehow the pirate ship was successfully maneuvering with the sails at full billow. This pirate captain, laughing insanely as he decimated the English galleon, must have decided that he was not going to allow a storm to interfere with his greedy lust for more English cargo. Dead passengers meant more bounty for him.

Salvo after salvo of cannon fire shattered the English hull, splintering the masts and the side of the ship. The sound was deafening. If the storm did not kill the English, those savage cannon blasts surely would.

It is surreal to watch what appears to be an

on-going battle and realize that the English ship, her passengers, and crew are already dead. You know that there is nothing that you can do to help them survive in their time. The horror for me lies in the understanding that for these people, the act of drowning, of being blasted, and the experience of dying is taking place repeatedly, seemingly without end, for hundreds of years.

Now I understand why Colleen had a headache: the ghost in the green wool dress, who was with her, had suffered a fatal head wound. Her problems breathing were based entirely on the sensation of the many ghosts drowning in a chilling ceaseless gurgling cycle. She felt the fatigue of the ghosts' exhaustion at endlessly fighting unsuccessfully for survival. However, I was not sure what or which ghost was causing my friend's stomach problems.

Answering Their Prayer

As the agonized screams continued, I began shifting the energy of the scene. I cannot change the history of this moment, but I can change the dire circumstances of these souls by requesting Divine assistance to stop the action so that the individuals no longer have to keep reliving these terrible moments. It's like sending a shock wave though a situation and bringing the 'stuck' repeating action to a final stop. This instantly caused this seemingly eternal moment to cease.

Angels assisted each soul. All were wrapped in Divine blankets, which offered them the beginnings of spiritual healing. Finally, I can now speak to them and find out how this appalling situation came to be. The young, redheaded woman seemed to be representing the 150 or so souls in front of me.

"Finally, we're in a safe place. I'm sure we can continue our journey to the new world. Once we dry off and you help us to dry land, we'll be able to find our way to the Jamestown settlement. Thank you so much."

Her powerful Irish brogue was so thick that I could barely understand her. Her hair, which now appeared to be drying, was a stunning red. I guessed her age to be about twenty-five, but she could have been younger. Rail thin, her salt-water saturated clothes hung on her body like entombing weights. Her green wool dress was without adornment; nor was there any comb or ribbon, that held back that now drying crimson hair. She didn't even have a shawl or sweater against the cold. She looked at me hopefully.

"Um, you're welcome. What's your name? How'd you come to be on this vessel?"

"I'm Eileen, and we're indentured servants going to work in the New World. The storm came upon us so suddenly we barely had a chance to get the sails down before the storm thrashed us. The rain was so bad, the sky was so dark, we were afraid we would hit the rocks, but we trusted our captain. Then, out of nowhere came the pirates.

"Where is this place? Why do you look so different from everyone else? Are these angels you have brought to help us? I expected to see the shore, not angels. I'm so confused. What's happened to us?"

I have often pondered what it is like to have someone bluntly tell you that you're dead, that all of your longings are over, and all of your dreams are dashed. . .

". . .we all died. It's my fault."

"You died, we all died. It's my fault. I should never have lowered the sails, but you have to understand I didn't want the masts to snap. I'm so sorry! I didn't see the pirates coming. I had too much weight on board to easily maneuver the ship and no real way to take evasive action once the sails were down. If I hadn't taken the sails down, we might have evaded the pirates but lost the masts and keeled over into the sea. What should I have done? I tried to protect the people in my care, but we died. We died! All of us! I lost my crew, my passengers, cargo, and my own life."

He grew introspective for a moment,

gaining composure to explain the rest of the sordid story.

"I watched the storm blow itself out. Eventually both ships sank as I watched, powerless to help anyone including myself. And then I was alone.

"Alone drifting at sea on a piece of the wreckage of my once proud ship. A quick death is so much more merciful than what happened to me. I was already exhausted but somehow, I kept holding on. I remember reviewing the crossing. What could I have done differently? The faces of the men, the women and all those small children who were always hungry on my ship endlessly haunted me: food was so scarce. All of us were slowly starving at sea and then the pirates finished us off.

"Then I remembered hearing the passenger's voices when the pirates came; they were so afraid, and they looked to me to save them. I failed them. I was blown into the water by one of the many cannon blasts, but I didn't die.

"Once I was in the water, I grabbed onto a piece of wood and watched as both ships sank. Immediately the nausea hit me, that sick feeling that comes from total failure as a human being. Within a day, the hunger gripped me like it was ripping out my stomach. I had so little strength. I was dying from the inside out. The pain grew. I swelled up horribly. The storm left and there was only the glare of the sun and the drying feeling of the salt water. Death was slow and tortuous. . . I don't remember the exact moment of my death. I guess the difference is that I recognized that death was my only companion on that piece of wood, and I think I eventually let go and slipped beneath the waves.

"Once I left my body, I tried to find the dead passengers. They had no idea that we all died. I watched them still hoping for help, oblivious to the facts of their new reality. This is all my fault."

His raspy voice was heavy with leaden guilt, agonizing emotional pain and the feeling of total despair. He was obviously the captain of the English galleon. His appearance was so startling that I caught my breath in horror. There were no more brightly polished brass buttons on his official uniform, only a few tattered shreds of blue material remained. His hat was gone, the hat that so clearly defines the rank and responsibility of any Naval officer in time and place.

He must have once been a very handsome man but in this moment all I saw was a horribly disfigured face. The swelling that comes from unrelenting sun at sea had rendered his face a hideous red. His eyes were swollen shut and his hair that may once have been mostly grey, was matted and limp. Starvation is so deceptive. This man would have looked large but only his cracking skin held his bones together.

He was feeling the guilt every conscientious captain feels when he loses his ship and incurs such an enormous loss of life. No matter what he did, they were all going to perish.

"Captain, you are understandably feeling the weight of all of these people. You are overwhelmed with the guilt of this loss of life. Why did the Admiralty let this ship travel alone? Did you want to make this journey alone?"

"No." He said flatly. I felt an instant flash of rage; disgust crossed his swollen face.

"No, usually we have an escort ship, with full cannon on board to defend us. I begged the Admiralty to send a fast frigate, a Corvette, or a Corsair with us for protection, but they said that they were shorthanded and couldn't spare one. I told them that you don't sail the waters off Carolina without an escort because there are just too many pirates, but they didn't believe me. Maybe they did believe me. Maybe there really weren't enough frigates. I begged them. I delayed departure but to no avail. I was ordered to take these people and their families to the New World with no protection.

"I was nervous about taking so many

people across the Atlantic without an escort. Plus, I barely had enough food on board to make the journey. We hit one storm after the other and food went over the side and people began to starve. As each day went on, there was less and less food. Once we began to sink, my passengers didn't have the strength to even try to swim. When the cannon hit us broadside, the cold water immediately flooded the spaces and people below decks. You have to understand that this happened at night and there was so much confusion. We never saw them coming. I had no place to take my ship and no way to take evasive action. I couldn't outrun him; I had no power! I'm so sorry. How can God forgive me for this? I'm the Captain and although I died with my shipmates, what comfort is there in that? At least, though, I know that the pirate ship captain didn't get what he wanted. At least I saw it happen before I died."

"What happened?"

"The pirate ship captain was laughing at our peril. The storm was so bloody fierce and yet there he was still firing away, taunting us. Bet he was French. He was just blasting us to Hell, but I know he got there first. Between the cannon blasts, the storm, and the wind, I glimpsed him in one crescendo lightning flash, a light blast that seemed to last many seconds. I saw him as he lost his balance, fell overboard, and was crushed under his own ship. He got what he deserved." He ended this discourse flatly as if karma was awkwardly served by the pirate captain's ignominious demise.

He dropped his head. Beyond him I could see his passengers in dripping clothes, beginning to feel the energy of eternal life start to return to them. The angels began quietly crossing them over one by one. Families met them. Hope crossed their faces as they felt the glorious embrace of the light.

"Eileen, do you now understand that you died that night? Are you ready to cross into that welcoming light?"

"I had such hopes for this new life. Will I ever get a chance to see the new world? Is it a wonderful place? I'm so sad that I never got a chance to see it."

"Once you cross over to the other side, the Light Beings there will help you to understand what happened here. And yes, the New World is truly an amazing place. Perhaps in some future life, you will be able to return here."

She looked back at me with tragic longing and that crushing fatigue that comes from such a catastrophic experience, and then she slipped away into the light. I turned to the ship's captain, who did not seem to be making any move toward that Light Bridge to the Heaven World.

"Captain, it's time."

"How can God forgive me? How? If I can't forgive myself, how can I expect God to forgive me? And all those people you just sent over that bridge; how will they ever forgive me?

"Do you know what it's like to see your own people die? Watching their bodies get blown up, watching young men and women holding on desperately to their children and their babies, drown because they had no hope of escaping the hold of the ship? The vision of this will haunt me for eternity. Maybe hell is where I belong. . ."

I turned and heard several very English voices interrupt him.

"No Captain! We won't be blamin' you, sir. This wasn't your fault. We respected your decision. You had to lower the sails. You tried to save us all, you did. We all forgive you, sir. Don't be punishin' yourself, now, sir, there's no need. We know you did the right thing. You're a fine captain, you are, the best. It's been an honor, Captain, an honor serving with you. Come with us."

I turned to this most honorable man.

"No, Captain. They're right, hell is not where you belong. Forgiveness is inherent in the very nature, the essence of God. Forgiveness is the hope that we can learn from what has happened. As you leave with this heavenly escort, and your loyal crewmembers, you will be able to see how all the events unfolded. You will get to see that in every moment, your first, last and constant intention was the safety of your passengers and crew. God knows that. That's all that matters. Death comes to all of us, sometimes sooner, sometimes later. We will get another opportunity at life. What matters now was what was in your heart in life. Come. Take the angel's hand. It's all right. It's time for this catastrophic event to finally be over."

He looked back at me with immense sadness in his eyes as he took the angel's outstretched hand and met the welcoming smiles of his crewmates.

And then the scene was gone, and only the sea as it looks today was visible. I then offered this area of the Atlantic healing so that the energy of this tragedy could be cleansed.

Epilogue

Once the ghostly Eileen, the ship's captain and all the ghosts of this watery scenario were assisted to the crossover bridge to the Heaven World, Colleen's fatigue ceased. Her headache vanished and she could breathe freely again. Her stomach also stopped feeling 'crawly,' a probable result of feeling the gnawing of the captain's stomach as he slowly starved to death. She was correct to suspect that she had a soul with her, but she could never have imagined how many souls had unknowingly connected to her. In her case the unfortunate side effect of being so psychic and so sensitive to ghosts was that she took on the physical manifestations of what the ghost was feeling. She was wise to ask for assistance in this situation.

This Captain's vessel was one of the thousands of passenger ships that plied the sea from England to the colonial settlements. I guessed by the type of ship that this life-shattering battle took place sometime in the last decades of the 1600s. Every single European colonist who settled in the Americas had to get here by three-masted ship, or frigate. The crossing took anywhere from five to seven weeks depending on weather, pirates, and general sailing conditions such as having enough wind to make sufficient nautical miles a day.

Disease, starvation, endless seasickness, and death in childbirth took so many lives; it is often a wonder that anyone survived the voyage. Food was a chronic issue since with the moist sea air, mold was an on-going problem and people were often sickened from the food itself.

Additionally, for the entire coast of the Americas, pirates were a constant threat and the English usually sent escort ships, but apparently not in this case.

I did not see any pirates in the group making the Divine crossing. I am only allowed to assist those souls presented to me. Where these pirates were, who found and assisted them, I do not know.

This is an example of two types of ghosts: Eileen, who had no idea she had died and kept reliving the last harrowing moments of her death, and the ship's Captain, who knew that he lost them all and was held in a hell of his own making because of his towering guilt. Crossing him over gave him the hope of a new life.

Perhaps the 'Graveyard of the Atlantic' is called that because so many people perished there that that section of the sea became in consistent resonance with death. Consider that since 1526, over 1,000 ships have perished in this part of the Atlantic off the coast of the Carolinas. There is no specific estimate of the actual number of souls lost here. Suffice it to say that they number in the tens of thousands. May God bless and keep them all.

Marjorie May

My clients, the Dickersons, always ask me to help them to clear their new house when they move. Sometimes it is a brand-new house, although there is no 'new' anymore, there is only ancient land where many thousands of people have lived or crossed or farmed. They live in Newport News, Virginia, an old city with quaint houses. Their area was not heavily populated until around the late 1940s or 1950s. Theirs was, and is, a neighborhood of quiet streets, mostly without sidewalks, just grass until the various yards abruptly meet the curb. Crab grass boldly dominates, always challenging the asphalt unless the homeowners diligently keep it in check from ultimately devouring the street.

Azaleas are in bloom; elegant maples grace and shade the wide street. Gracious older Southern neighborhoods have that typical green canopy of trees that softens the age of homes.

People are friendly and curious. Neighbors

know each other, what church they attend and what the husband does for a living. People mow their own lawns and tend to their own yards. That was the feeling I received as I studied this neighborhood. The couple's house appeared to be on a street of houses built in the late 1950s and was constructed with red brick and white siding. It was not a large house, roughly three bedrooms, living room, kitchen and two bathrooms. The detached garage in the back, today, was more of a garden shed than a garage.

She met me at the door, an emaciated figure with blackened, sunken eyes and a determined, steady gaze. I knew she had been expecting me.

The Deacon

Her name was Marjorie May and she looked to be in her mid-thirties. She might have had pretty hair, but her short dull blonde hair was mostly gone, almost as if she had had radiation poisoning. Her skin was gaunt. Every time I even think of her, I start to sneeze over and over as if this situation created an allergic reaction within me. Her formerly white nightgown was now terribly soiled.

I was curious to hear her narrative. She gave me the basics, some I could feel or sense, but somehow, I knew that there was going to be more to her story, more puzzles to solve.

34

Her husband's name was Zebulon, a pharmacist at the local drug store. He was also a deacon in their church, but she never said which church, only that he was a deacon. Obviously, something about his position in the church may have attracted her to him and, at the same time, terrified her. He was definitely an intimidating figure in her life: strong, dominant, and demanding.

She Knows She is Dead

Perhaps in a certain sense, death freed her to see what kind of man she married, giving herself permission to haunt his days as he had so brutally dominated hers. She was more than anxious to tell her story.

"He was that movie star ideal: tall, dark, brooding, and handsome in a somewhat dangerous, almost tantalizing way. Everything seemed to happen quickly. He swept me off my feet. I could feel his masked power on every date we had. His energy was overwhelming, almost like he consumed me with his personality. He ordered for me, helped me to make every decision. He told me he was crazy about me and there were moments when it felt like he was breathing in all my energy, my sense of who I was. But I doubted myself. I . . . I had never had anyone pay this much notice to me. Maybe I was starved for attention and he poured it on, poured it on me in a thousand ways. He bought me flowers, and we always went to the nicest restaurants. He spent hours telling me about his life, his dreams, and his plans for us.

"I remember hesitating inside, thinking that this was all happening so fast, too fast. Is it real? Is it right? I was excited but at the same time, there was this nagging warning light that I kept seeing in my heart . . . and I ignored it.

"I remember moments of pure fear before our rushed wedding. Those chilling moments would come out of nowhere like some demon appearing, instantly ready to lacerate my happiness. The closer I got to that wedding day, the more those attacks of terrifying dread crushed me. Sometimes the fear was so paralyzing that I threw up. Obviously, this was a warning I should have heeded but I felt like I was on a run-away freight train and that there was no stopping it.

"Zeb dismissed my fears when I tried to mention them. Maybe there was a part of me that knew this was a hideous mistake, knew that somehow Zeb was not the wonderful person he seemed. Why didn't I listen to those feelings? Why?

"We were married after only a few months in a small wedding in the church. Since Zeb was a deacon, we had a church full of people, most of whom I did not know. Zeb picked out my wedding dress and every detail about the wedding. I thought that meant that he cared about me, that it made me special. At times, I wanted to make some decisions; it was the 1950s after all, women were able to do more. But not me. I showed up and put on the gown he bought. Someone handed me a bouquet of flowers that I didn't pick out. I couldn't tell you what color they were or if they even smelled nice. The ring he put on my finger (that he selected), eventually felt like an iron shackle on my soul."

Aloneness and Isolation

Marjorie continued with her sad dissertation.

"I didn't have a family. I was an only child, so after my parents died when I left high school, I was on my own. I went to secretarial school and I got a job at the pharmacy where Zeb worked, typing up the prescriptions. I didn't really even have any friends. After I lost my parents, I felt that no one could understand that much grief. There was no one to confide in, who could guide or counsel me. I don't think you are supposed to feel completely alone on your wedding day – but I did. Another deacon walked me down the aisle and gave me away, gave me away into this life of perpetual bondage. No slave, no captive ever had a more elegant or deceptive sendoff.

"I guess I should have noticed how controlling he was, but the wedding, our being together seemed to happen so fast that I . . ."

Her voice trailed away as if the memory of that last day of freedom, of health and happiness flooded her heart every time she thought of it.

"Did you work outside of your home? Did you have any children? Did you want children? Was it discussed?"

"Even in the modern age, a proper wife in the 1950s didn't work outside of the home. I brought it up, but Zeb said my working would disgrace him. He made me feel terrible when I brought it up. I was a good secretary before we were married. Yes, I would have loved a child, but there was a part of me that knew that I could not do that to a child. There was no way I wanted to bring a child into that home – with that loathsome church deacon. I think I willed myself to not get pregnant. And then later, I was so sick. . ."

She sighed a deep sigh as if she could see back in time when she began to give up.

"We hadn't been married very long when the beatings started. At first, we went to church together every Sunday and I also went with him when he had to go to church meetings during the week. But once he started beating me, my bruises showed so badly and I was so humiliated I could not go any longer. Zeb would tell me that I couldn't show my shameful face in church. He said that the bruises would show people how bad I was. If I looked or smiled at someone, and he saw this simple friendly act of being gracious, I was beaten. If someone reached to shake my hand and I responded, when we got home, I was beaten. He beat me if the house wasn't perfect. If he had a bad day at the pharmacy, he beat me. I knew when it would start because this look would come over him, it would devour him as his monster emerged. He slapped me, punched and kicked me. The monster hid in public, but at home, or prison as I came to see it, the monster unleashed his wrath on me at every opportunity. How could I expose a child to this?"

"I know you said you had no family at the wedding, but did you have family elsewhere who could come and get you, who could rescue you? Surely there was someone you could tell?"

"Maybe that's why he picked me, because I had no one. My family died. I had no siblings, anyone to be there for me. There was no one for me to go to." She said this in a voice above a whisper.

"Surely your church had a lady's auxiliary and they would have wanted you to participate. I know that often, church women try to welcome the wives of deacons, what happened when these ladies came by to visit?"

"I would have loved to have left the house, been part of the activities of the church, but if anyone came over to visit, Zeb said that I was sick, and he turned them away. He was rude. I was humiliated. I was absolutely his prisoner. I couldn't drive. Lots of women in the fifties learned to drive, but Zeb wouldn't allow it. It was too far to walk anywhere, and Zeb would have killed me if I had tried it. I fantasized about how to leave him, but I had not a penny to my name.

"I was injured most of the time. At some moments, at that point when I was close to death, I had trouble walking at all. I was in pain all the time. If I cried out, murmured, or even moaned, he would beat me. He was the devil incarnate."

"Was there anything that brought you any hope or joy?"

"My only respite was working on the flowers in my yard. I sent for gardening catalogs and found solace in the earth itself. Our yard was as beautiful as I could make it, as much as I could do when I didn't have broken bones trying to heal. Sometimes I spent all day in the back yard in the gardening shed potting plants. Sometimes my neighbor, Sam, would come over to talk, but I was always very careful to make sure that Zeb had left for work. I was terrified that he would kill Sam if he saw me talking to him. I was never allowed to have a friend at all. Sam was retired."

She continued.

"Sam saw what was happening to me and offered to take me to the police, to a hospital. Once he actually got me to go to a hospital in Norfolk so that we wouldn't be in Newport News. They bandaged me up and gave me pills for the pain. They set my broken bones. Sam begged me to go to the police, but I refused. No one would do anything because he was a deacon; I knew that to the depth of my core. I was so terrified of Zeb harming Sam that I asked them to wrap my arm instead putting it in a cast, which would have kept the bones from moving. The pain was so great as those bones moved, that I passed out at one point, but I could not go home with a cast on my arm."

My Murderer

"I knew he would kill me; it was just a matter of time. The fear I had on my wedding day became my only constant companion.

"Then his behavior changed suddenly, as if someone turned a switch: Zeb stopped beating me. He wasn't necessarily nice to me, and several times when he started to beat me, he stopped. This made me extremely nervous.

He seemed more evil than usual. A chill went down my already ever-frozen spine. It was as if he wanted my bruises to recover so that no one could see them, and it petrified me.

"As my bruises began to fade and my bones mended, I began to look normal again. Zeb told me he was worried about my thyroid and he said he would bring home medicine to 'help' me. I was terrified that he would poison me. I made up my mind that if there were pills that I would secretly spit them out. If it were a liquid, I wouldn't drink it.

"But he never overtly gave me any medicine. All I knew was that, as time went by, I went from healing and feeling human again to wishing death would come. I knew he was poisoning me, but I didn't know how. He did all the grocery shopping. I couldn't get to a store to make sure my food was safe. I hesitated to eat at all, but I was so hungry. After each meal the pain would come. It was a horrible choice: starve to death or allow myself to be steadily poisoned. I had no one to confide in and I felt absolutely trapped.

"Eventually, I lost the will to live as the stabbing knife-pain in my stomach continued until I begged for death. I vomited non-stop. My hair fell out. I never changed the smelly soiled housedress I was wearing. One day, blessedly, I rolled over in bed and died. I had been dead for several days when Zeb finally called the police to report that I had died. They took my body away. There was a funeral. Only the other deacons came. I had no friends."

He Remarries

"After my death, I followed my husband around to see what he was doing and discovered that he had a new focus for his evil, one of the women who worked at the pharmacy. She knew he was widowed, and he was young enough to remarry.

"Barely six months went by, scarcely a whisper in time since I had died, before he married her. This time, though, she had a family. The first time he hit her, she got into her car (the one he had wanted her to get rid of) and fled to her family. She had the marriage annulled.

"Word of the annulment spread throughout the church and Zeb wasn't a deacon anymore because she told his church that he beat her, and she showed them the bruises. He was humiliated at losing his deaconship. I was worried he would kill this poor girl, but he didn't. He wasn't ashamed; he just slunk away. He never remarried.

"I know that I'm stuck where I am, in this hell that is death and this death that is still hell, although it is good to finally get to tell someone."

"Did Sam see what happened to you?"

"I don't know. He probably saw the coroner remove my battered body. What could he do? He never saw Zeb beat me. No one did. Zeb was clever. I'm glad he didn't marry for a third time, and I'm glad every day that we didn't have a child."

"Are you still in pain? Would you like something for the pain? I also have fresh clean clothes here and a warm blanket to soothe your tired broken bones."

While she was beginning to brighten slightly at having clean clothes and relief from that unrelenting pain, I brought in an angel to take her hand and help her to cross over into the light. The light heals you to your very core, to every cell and enables you to feel hope again. As she crossed over, I could see that her hair had been restored and her body was glowing. I could see that love returned to her soul as her beloved parents met her and welcomed her home.

Epilogue

When I shared this story with my clients, at first, they felt that this explained the feeling of a presence out of the corner of their eye. As I continued telling this sad tale of brutality, they finally stopped me. In a strange twist of fate, they were stunned because they bought the house from the grandson of a man named

Sam. He had been the only owner. The Dickersons and I believe that Marjorie must have eventually found refuge in Sam's house because she met me at the Dickerson's' house. The house next door is the house that Marjorie lived in and has the potting shed in the back and the gorgeous gardens. We discussed the weird anomaly at length. The ghost was in their house and yet she was telling me about the house next door, the house in which she lived and died.

Marjorie never mentioned that she went to live with Sam as a ghost and was haunting the house he lived in instead of the house in which she had died. Perhaps she saw the light and the goodness of Sam and, while she may have watched her horrible husband at a distance, she never wanted to live there anymore. We will never know.

The Battle Royal

Scientists know that the rings of a tree are individual records of what type of weather has occurred in a given area. The tree logs within its rings how its life has evolved by recording the energy that was available to it throughout its lifetime.

Psychics can also tap into the spiritual energy of a tree and catch a glimpse of what happened in the past because trees are like anchors in time. If the intuitive encounters a ghost, often times a very ancient nearby tree can offer greater insight into what happened to that soul. Trees are also unwilling spectators to unspeakable acts of violence. Some trees are used as methods of death, and others never grow correctly because of the traumatic energy that permeated the ground in a particular year.

I believe that the roots of the tree absorb the energy that is surrounding them throughout various times in the tree's history. Tree rings faithfully record more than merely weather and rainfall but remember with quiet dignity the trials and triumphs of those who lived and died nearby. Perhaps that was the case in the roughly 300-year-old oak tree that I encountered one hot June day in Colonial National Historical Park in Yorktown, Virginia. I had never been to Yorktown, Virginia, but while visiting family there, we decided to visit this impressive historical landmark. We stopped at Redoubts 9 and 10.

Once I saw the Redoubts, those often hastily built protection berms, I knew that there were probably going to be a hefty number of ghosts waiting – for something – and that is if they even realized that they were dead.

Sentinels of Time

Several gigantic oak trees graced this area on that hot summer day. I suspected that most of them were planted by some hapless squirrel after a major battle since these trees were between two and three hundred years old. The wide girth of their magnificent trunks dwarfed visitors. Their generous green canopy of rustling, swaying leaves provided welcome shade and invited me to linger with them, and I could see their gnarled roots spreading many yards in all directions. Any trees in that area would have been felled and used to fortify the redoubt during those early Revolutionary War years. I felt that the tree was still a sentinel in time even though it appeared to be planted after the battle. Nonetheless, the energy of the battle would have been absorbed into the sapling root structure, thereby creating a connection to the past. I immediately noticed that as I laid my hands on the tree, and closed my eyes, I became in resonance with this living structure.

It takes a few minutes to sift through the years, to see the area, to feel the passage of time and to locate that moment exerting the greatest influence on this currently, deceptively, peaceful battlefield.

Suddenly, there is no more peace: there's a grimy mist of smoke and death that hangs over everything. I'm having trouble discerning at first and then I hear men screaming in pain, officers shouting orders over the din of muzzleloaders going off, and the unmistakably acrid smell of gunpowder filling the air as cannons are fired.

I began to see a battle raging in this clearing by the redoubt, an entire army of ghosts still fighting each other. It's a bit unnerving to be standing in 2012 and be able to see an entire battle raging in front of you.

Finally, a young boy with fiery, long red hair who looked to be between 12 and 14 years of age approached me with a surprised look on his face.

"Is it over yet? You don't look like the others, is it over yet?" This young man spoke with a decided Scottish brogue.

"Is what over yet? What's happening here? What's your name, soldier?"

"My name's Private McDougal - Mathew, they call me Mathew. I'm a fife player, fighting the French."

"Well Mathew, it's over, and it has been over for a very long time. Tell me, son, how did you come to be here, did you enlist in the English Army?"

"You mean there's no more battle going on? But how come I can still see soldiers fighting and dying?"

"You can still see them because, just like you, they don't realize that this battle ended badly for all of you. When each of you fell, you didn't understand that you died, so you all simply continued doing what you were doing that half-second before you died. How did you come to be here in the first place?"

"I'm dead? (Pause)

"I'm dead. I - I had no idea. I didn't realize what death would feel like, that I wouldn't even notice it. I wanted to live a longer life, to explore this new land, to see Indians. I had hopes. I wanted an adventure, although once we left England, there were moments at sea - where, you know, - that we all hoped for death.

I always felt death was near me, almost like I could touch it. Guess I hoped it wouldn't touch me.

"None of us enlisted. One day this man in a uniform came to our orphanage in Scotland and told us that we were joining the English Army and that we were leaving for the New World in a few days. We didn't know whether to be excited or not. The orphanage was pretty bad, and we had no future, but we had each other. We thought maybe this conscription was at least some type of adventure. The trip from the Highlands to the coast of England was by coach. It was becoming cool when we left. I was already afraid of how cold it would be at sea.

"The ship, with her tall masts, looked strong and safe. I began to be a bit excited about the voyage, hoping that this would turn out to be an adventure after all. I'm tall for fourteen and I wanted to learn how to climb the masts and scout for land. I had dreams of what the future could be; so did all the lads.

"We didn't know how horrible the crossing would be for us. None of us had ever been to sea before. We knew we'd drown if we went overboard since none of us could swim. There were 25 of us when we started. The ocean was rough every day and we all retched so much that a couple of the younger boys died. Some of them were as young as ten years old. The

Ghost Stories from the Ghosts' Point of View

Admiralty didn't care about their age and the orphanage didn't want to have to feed us. The younger ones were weaker, I guess. You can't eat if you can't keep it down. I had never seen anyone buried at sea before. No one cared about boys like us. I guess no one cared about us in life or death. Each dead boy was one less mouth to feed. (Mathew looking away, seems to wipe his eye, looks down, embarrassed by the emotion that rises up.) I wanted to cry, you know, but I didn't want no one to see me cry. These were good lads. I didn't know if they died from fear or seasickness."

He pauses again, feeling that he was the only one who grieved his young shipmates.

"We were so excited to see land since it had been so many long weeks at sea. I hoped that we were safe, but before we knew it, we encountered a French galleon off the coast of Virginia.

"We were terrified that the French would destroy our ship after we had come such a long way. I remember watching the French ship light off their cannon against us. When the cannon balls hit us broadside, I watched men fly through the air and die right in front of me. I – I had no idea that death could be so sudden, so violent . . . I didn't know what to do. The captain was barking orders to the helmsman to try to out-maneuver the French, but it was going really badly for us. We were caught by surprise. The Resolute, our ship, was wheeling and rolling and we could barely hold on. The smell of gunpowder was heavy in the air; the French outgunned us. I figured we were all going to get blown up or drowned for sure right then."

"When I thought that all was lost."

"I couldn't believe it: when I thought that all was lost, a huge fog bank rolled in and we escaped the French. We were able to slip away and then we found safe harbor. However, I could see that our ship was so badly damaged that I knew in my heart that I wasn't ever gonna' be able to return to Scotland. I couldn't believe we made it here. So many times, I thought surely, we would die from storms, sea sickness and battles."

"Do you know what year it is?"

"It's 1781, why do you ask?"

"Just curious, please continue. How did you come to be here in this place, in this darkness with a battle raging all around you?"

"When we were aboard ship, on the HMS Resolute, we knew we had to have some useful skill once we made landfall, so one of the sailors taught me how to play the fife. He said it might help me to survive longer once we got here. I hoped he was right. He was the first kind person I had met on the ship and he seemed to want to help me. He taught my friend John, how to play a drum. So, we were in the Fife and Drum corps and the soldiers kept us behind the lines. They treated me, and some of the other boys, like their mascots. I felt like they were trying to keep us alive. The senior officers told us to stay behind the redoubt, that we would be safer there and to keep our heads down. I was grateful that we could stay there. It was like this big earthen wall. The soldiers had built this before we got there, using trees, earth, anything they could use, to create a barrier to the barrage of French gunfire.

"But as the days went on and more and more battles raged, some of the soldiers were concerned that we would become the youngest fighters. So, they taught all of us boys how to shoot a muzzleloader because I guess they thought that with all the casualties we were suffering that we would have to start fighting alongside them soon. I guess they figured we had to have some way to defend ourselves if all the other soldiers died . . . died in their bright red coats.

"That muzzleloader was so heavy that it took two of us to even lift it and we realized that we had to help each other to load it, and then to tamp it down. There was so little ammunition that we couldn't practice shooting and we knew that every shot had to count. I didn't know that within days of them showing us how, that we would be fighting too. After the last battle we had at least 150 dead and the sergeant told us we had to help with the next fight. It looked to me like the French had greater numbers of just about everything, troops, supplies, and ammunition. I didn't know how we were going to defeat them. How could they just keep comin' and comin'?

"I'm not a soldier. I play the fife. I didn't know how to fight the French, Indians, or colonists. I didn't understand what we were fighting for or why we were all killing each other. I was in combat for the first time and I actually fired a shot and I killed one of the Frenchmen.

"I play the fife."

"I play the fife; I'm not a killer. You have to understand that when I killed that man, I was horrified that he died. Then a French soldier attacked me and shot at me with his pistol. I – I guess I thought he missed me.

"I see this bright glow over there. Is that for me? It's been night for so long here, I guess I never noticed that the dawn never came. Is the darkness I thought was night, really death? I thought I was still fighting that prissy Frenchman and that the day turned to night.

"I'm a fife player but I guess even fife players die just like everybody else. Are you here to help me?"

"Yes, son, I'm here to help all of you. You aren't the only one who had no idea that the battle was over. I would imagine that all of you thought that the day had just turned to night. But it didn't. You all died within a few days' time of each other. I've brought in my own soldiers, spiritual soldiers to help you all cross over into that bright glow over there. It's okay. Put this warm cloak on your tired shoulders. I've got cloaks for all the rest of these battle-weary souls too. The war is officially over."

Mathew looked at me briefly with wonder and hope in his deep blue eyes and then he willingly crossed over with his angel. I then turned my attention to the rest of the French, English and Continental soldiers who seemed to be surprised to find that their guns no longer worked. When the soldiers saw the growing light of the Divine, their guns and swords dropped to the ground and their hands went limp beside their bodies. A stark reality arrived in their souls. They began to come to terms with the certainty that they were dead as the warmth seemed to envelope them all. Finally, they all began to realize that whatever they thought was the end, was now a bright beginning.

I do not know who met Mathew McDougal

when he crossed over, much less any of the other 25 young lads who journeyed with him to the new world on that English vessel. They were orphans, everyone with no one to love them, and no one to care that they would never come home. Yet, as they crossed that light bridge, I saw them welcomed home, glimpsed smiles cross their excited faces and watched as arms outstretched, they fell into warm embraces.

Epilogue

The date of this particular battle was October 14th, 1781. The blood of several thousand men and boys saturated the ground, near where this future tree would grow. The energy of the blood of the fallen is literally taken up through the roots of the tree. The saga of the battle for independence left casualties through many time periods. When the earth has been this traumatized, when death hangs this heavy it is critical to offer healing to the earth and to transmute the energy of man's mindless slaughter of other human beings.

Predecessor energy is powerful and affects those living today because it exists at the same time as the time that we think it is existing, today. Those soldiers believed that it was nighttime. None of them had any idea that death had come for them. This is the reason that all battlefields should be kept as public parks. No one should live on an area that has had this volume of human blood spilled on the land. That much blood, the energy of severe suffering, fear, violence, and the trauma of battle are toxic for the earth. Even clearing it, while it helps in a sense, the land is still hallowed because the energy of death is still lingering even to this very day.

If you happening to be visiting a battlefield, then make it a point to get out *The Crossing Over Prayer©* or use *The Crossing Over Prayer Book©*. Specifically look for *Prayer 24. The Crossing Over Prayer for War Dead.*

Say this prayer at least three times until you feel a specific 'shift' – something so subtle, so gentle you may not be sure you even felt it but it will be there.

If you do this, I would love to hear from you.

The Toothache

The following case came as a call I received about a routine trip to the dentist, but the aftermath of the experience was anything but routine. No anesthesia was involved. No one almost died. This was not an energy story. The client is a happy person. Things went well for the client in the dentist's chair. Everything should have been just fine. She was only there for a few minutes – but afterwards, things were anything but fine.

The 3rd Eye Headache

My teenage client, Callie, called me with a terrible headache. She said that earlier that morning she had gone to the dentist to have sealants placed on three of her teeth. She was only there a few minutes for this painless procedure. But the headache started while she was in the dentist's office and lasted into the evening. She confirmed that she did not receive any anesthesia during the office visit.

By the time she called me, she said that she had tried everything to get rid of the headache and nothing had worked. No pill, powder, or remedy made a dent in the unrelenting pain that seemed to be focused on the center of her forehead, the area known as her third eye.

It is unusual to call a psychic when you have a headache, but in this case, the client has had previous experience with these types of headaches: 3rd eye headaches usually mean that someone is with her, someone she cannot see. She asked me to 'take a look' and see if she was correct. While Callie wanted her headache to stop, at the same time, she had a genuine desire to help whoever may be attached to her.

"Was God punishing me?"

There are ghosts who want to convey a message or a warning. Others want help understanding not only what happened to them, but who also want to leave the depressing location or situation in which they find themselves. Some of the saddest ones are seeking help with the pain that sometimes lingers with them after death. And every so often, that pain is deeply emotional.

As I begin to work with my client, it isn't long before I realize that she is correct. Almost immediately, I see a waif of a young girl, standing in the room next to my client.

"Can you see me? I come to help her, your friend. I had to warn her. Oh, I forgot my manners, I'm Sally Ann."

Sally Ann's clothes are dirty and faded; her blue patterned dress is worn thin and there are holes in her skirt. Her dirty, stringy brown hair falls below her shoulders and is covered in pieces of hay. As she begins to talk, I instantly get the impression that we are in the 1930s, the height of the depression.

"Why do you need to warn Callie? Is she in danger from something?"

"I'm – I'm not real sure, but somethin' bad happened to me at that there dentist. My head hurt somethin' awful. It was so bad, I cried and cried. Then I died. I come to warn your friend to be real careful there, that's all. Just that. But maybe, maybe it was my fault that I died."

She shivers inwardly as if the cold she feels iced her soul. I hope the warm blanket I have draped around her extremely thin, shivering, shoulders will begin to warm her.

"Honey, why would your death be your fault? Can you tell me what happened to you?"

"I don't rightly know what happened. I don't remember her – my mama. Papa says that she run off when I was just a little thing, probably 'cause Papa and me were just bad people. Papa says it's how God punishes people: they make your mama run off. Maybe I'm bad 'cause she didn't want to be my mama. Was God jus' punishin' me? Do you think that's what happened to me?"

She pauses here, as if the concept of this is intensely painful. Her father's endless pronouncement that God is punishing them must have been the only rationale he could think of, for why times are so hard for them, why they are starving to death and probably why his daughter is in so much pain. The glaring absence of her mother haunts her day and night. The aching longing to be embraced by her mother's love is her deepest heartache.

"Sally Ann, I don't think God is punishing you. Can you tell me a bit more about how you happened to be at the dentist's office?"

"Things is bad, real bad. We ain't got no place to live. Papa, he's a handy man. He fixes stuff. There's a farmer who lets us sleep in his barn. I don't mind sleepin' in the sweet hay. I got used to the smell of them horses and the cow that the family has. But they don't have much and they don't share their food with us. We're hungry all the time.

"I'm kinda sure papa loves me, but he don't say much. He tries to be good to me but he's kinda gruff. There ain't much work. Folks can't pay for fixin' broke stuff. Sometimes papa trades his work for food. He's tired all the time. So am I. It's cold now. We're always cold.

"You got to understand that I try real hard to be a good girl. But no matter how hard I try, papa says that we must be real bad people for God to punish us like this, not lettin' us have food and barely shelter."

A Terrible Pain

"I don't rightly know how it happened, but I gets this terrible hurt in my mouth. I start to grab at my face and papa asks what's happenin' and I tell him how much my mouth hurts. He looks inside and says I need somethin' called a dentist. Then his face gets all red and angry. I'm thinking that we ain't got no money for no dentist. I don't rightly know what to do, 'cause the pain is just gettin' worse and worse.

"I bet if I had a mama she'd know what to do. You know, mamas know stuff about how to care for their kids. But I ain't got no mama.

"Finally, I'm layin' in the hay, and I can't get up the pain's so bad, so papa leaves and says he's goin' to try and get me some help. He's gone a good while. When he come back, he told me he traded work for help from a dentist and he picks me up off the floor of the barn, and we go see this man.

"I ain't never been in no dentist's office. I'm a'feared of him. I sat in his chair and he tells me to open my mouth real wide. But it hurts to open my mouth. He yells at me to open real wide. Then he reaches from behind him and comes at me with this here tool and yanks out my tooth. I think I went almost dead with the pain and musta' fell asleep. When I woke up, I felt this horrible hurt in my mouth. Then the pain stopped, but not for long.

"When we get back to the barn, I lay in the hay and then the blood starts to come from where my tooth used to be. Lots of blood. I start to swallow all of this blood. I'm so afraid. It's funny, as I'm bleedin', I stop feelin' hungry. Then the headache comes, so bad that I start to vomit and I'm vomiting blood. The headache's so bad I reckon I started to scream.

"Papa left and went back to that dentist. The dentist tells papa that he does teeth, not headaches. Papa come back to the barn and he sits by me. There ain't nothin' he can do fer me. He sits by me all night. I can sometimes see the sadness on his face as I'm cryin' and screamin' with the headache.

"Then I reckon I musta gone to sleep 'cause when I waked up I see papa holdin' me and he's cryn' real hard. As I'm standin' there watchin' him, I pretty much figured out that I died. I reckoned that papa was cryin' 'cause I died whilst he was a'holdin' me. I was real glad that I weren't alone when I died. I'm glad he was there."

"What happened when you died, after you

realized that you weren't in your body anymore, did your headache stop?"

"I reckoned I was a goner 'cause I could see papa holdin' me and then I didn't see him much after that and I was in all this blackness. Then I couldn't find papa no more, like he just weren't there no more. Then I started to get real a'feared. My headache still kinda' comes and goes. Now I ain't gots nobody to love me or tell me what to do next or help me with this pain."

"Is the punishing time over?"

"Sally Ann, honey, how did you happen to come upon my friend Callie? How did you find her and why did you come home with her?"

"I ain't rightly sure I know but I found myself wandering the blackness and I reckon I went back to that dentist office or close by. I ain't real sure how I found your friend, but she was in a dentist office, and she was young like, and I was a'feared for her. I wanted to warn her, tell her to git outta there 'cause bad stuff was gonna' happen to her!

"But she don't hear me, no one hears me, 'ceptin you. You're the first person come to talk to me in a real long time. . . Is your friend sick too?"

"No, my friend's not sick. She's just fine. My friend figured out that you were with her and that you might need help. Would you like some help with your headache? Are you finally feeling warmer?"

"Yes'm I surely would. That's a right fine shawl you put on me, but are ya' sure? I mean I ain't had no bath in nigh on forever. I don't want to be gettin' it dirty."

"I wouldn't be worried about that. And look, I've brought you a friend to help you feel better. See this lovely angel? She's just your age. She wants to take you home to God because you are more than worthy of His love. It's time for this pain, cold and loneliness to be over."

"Ma'am, you sure 'bout this? This angel, I guess you said that's what she is, is puttin' her hand in mine. But papa said that God was punishin' us. How come I feels so much better? Is the punishin' time over? I reckon I's still a'feared. Papa said that I would get punished worse iffin' I was to go to heaven. Now I reckon I don't rightly know what to do. Maybe I should stay here with your friend. At least now I know she ain't gonna' hurt me."

"Sally Ann, this angel is here for you. My friend, Callie, can no longer help you. It's time to let go of my living friend and allow yourself to enter the embrace of this glorious light. Dearest child, God loves you more than you can ever imagine, and it was never His intention that you suffer so. I know what your papa said, but he wasn't right. He was just a sad man who did the best he could with what he had, and he felt punished by the circumstances of his life. I'm so sorry for what has happened to you, for how much pain you have suffered. The suffering time is over.

"I want you to go with this angel into the Heaven World. There you will receive even more healing. It's okay. You're safe. Let go of Callie and allow yourself to be free of this darkness."

The angel looks at me brightly and signals that she is ready for the crossover. Then she smiles at Sally Ann as they skip across the light bridge as if they are two best friends finally reunited. I noticed in the distance across the bridge that there is a woman waiting to welcome Sally Ann home. I don't know who that is, perhaps a grandmother? As the scene closes, I watch this woman scoop Sally Ann up in a tremendous embrace.

Sometimes children and adults are confused when death comes, and it can be extremely helpful to request that an angel guide them to the Heaven World. This enables the child to heal from whatever caused his or her death. Unfortunately, no one did this initially for Sally Ann. She may have realized that death had come for her, but she had no idea how to find the light and leave the darkness.

Epilogue

I suspected that Sally Ann's teeth began to fall apart with the lack of nutrition: no calcium for teeth and bones, cold all the time, no teeth care whatsoever. They were lucky to eat at all. The father's constant insistence that they were being punished made them feel that they were not even worthy of life itself. I have no doubt that the loss his daughter confirmed to this man that he was absolutely being punished. While he may have been pretty rough around the edges, it is clear that he truly loved his daughter. He must have been devastated after she died, eternally blaming himself for his failings as her father.

The dentist, from what I was told, was a pretty heartless individual. Maybe the dentist had no pain medication, but his care for his charity case was abhorrent. He very probably did not sterilize his instruments. (Antibiotics were not in general use at this time, having only been discovered by Alexander Fleming in 1928. In fact, widespread use of antibiotics was not begun until 1941.)

Because the dentist was not getting cash, only work in trade, he did the bare minimum. Even in the 1930s, dentists knew that once you pull a tooth, you have to pack the socket so that the bleeding can stop, otherwise the patient could bleed to death. We will never fully know whether she bled to death or died from a combination of blood loss, and/or a stomach full of blood. Perhaps massive infection ferociously invaded her body, and septicemia eventually shut down all of her organs. Her headache after having her tooth pulled could have been due to the massive infection that quickly spread throughout her body and into her brain. Death came in a very short time.

I can only imagine how powerless her father must have felt. There was nothing he could do but rock her in his arms and feel her slip away from him, the only thing in the whole world he had left, the only one he ever truly loved and who had loved him unconditionally in return.

Chicken Wire

Predecessor Energy

P redecessor energy is exceptionally powerful. What makes the concept of predecessor energy so fascinating to understand is that the energy can follow a person and may not necessarily, be location specific.

That sounds pretty confusing, but think about this scenario: have you ever met a person who seemed obsessed by something, like, the Civil War? These are the guys who endlessly participate in the reenactments of various Civil War battles throughout the North and South. Perhaps they are reincarnated Civil War soldiers. The bitter irony is that even in their reenactments, they still die. No one saves them. They are dying again and again and again. The energy of the Civil War keeps following them. They usually live near a battleground site, although there are those who travel great distances to participate in the reenactments. These souls embody the concept of predecessor energy living within them. They each represent the predecessor and the energy itself.

Reenactments are not the only way that a person can experience predecessor energy, as the following story graphically depicts.

What if someone had a past life that was filled with so much violence, so horrific that the energy of that life never seems to leave him?

What if that past life predecessor energy was so powerful that it haunted the person without end?

What if this type of haunting was an emotional haunting, not something that you could say was outwardly supernatural?

What if the soul brought not only the horror of a tremendous past life into the present, but also the ghosts from that life? The person is the predecessor and the embodiment of the predecessor energy that he thought he had left behind.

The phenomenon is extremely rare and often difficult to fully comprehend. However, this highly unusual situation is often bizarre in its consequences for the person living in modern times. Such is the case of my friend Robert, living in Virginia Beach, Virginia.

Robert, a highly educated and sensitive man, is also a practicing homeopathic physician. He combines the scientific logic of medicine with an unusual abiding belief in the spiritual world, due to the curious otherworldly experiences he has encountered. His career choice has always seemed something of a conundrum to me: he seems to detest dealing with blood and infection. He has always appeared to me to be traumatized from some event somewhere in his distant past, not this lifetime, but from another time.

Hence, one afternoon I received a call from him requesting that I remote view his home to determine if it was haunted. He kept having this uneasy feeling and wanted me to clear anything or anyone who might be there. Who knew that this would turn out to be one of the most remarkable remote viewing situations I have ever experienced.

Navigating Through the Darkness

I began my remote view of Robert's home one evening, as most people would be drifting off to sleep. Energy is calmer at night and remote viewing is much easier at this time.

When I located his house in time and space, I found that there were massive clouds of blackness that were surrounding his home. I was unable to discern why there was so much blackness, only that it looked as if his house had been dipped in the darkness of hell.

I took a deep breath, gathered up my

courage and began navigating through the blackness. Exploring his house, I found total darkness inside his dwelling as well. When a location is this densely negative, I automatically ask angels for guidance and protection. It was impossible to immediately discern the source of this sooty darkness. I began my exploration of what I believed to be his modern-day home.

I initially observed an entryway with windows that should have let in light, but no light came from them. But I found I could not go farther because I was drawn to the left of the entryway by a long dark hallway with patches of light piercing the penetrating inky gloom. I knew Robert's house did not have a long dark hallway to the left in these modern 21st century times.

Momentarily, I felt stuck there. I hesitated. Was I truly stuck, or was it my own subconscious that did not want to face what I would be forced to see down that passageway? There was a growing ominous sense about this corridor: a grim reality that I felt loathe to face. This hallway space was in a different dimension. It was not part of Robert's house at all. I realized that I had slipped into a different stack of time, probably, a past time and I dreaded what I would find down that stretch of forbidding hallway.

In an effort to get my bearings, I looked

outside this corridor to what would have been the outdoors. There I found more smoky gloom, but in this suffocating energy I was able to faintly notice that 6″ above the ground was chicken wire – acres and acres of chicken wire as far as I could see. Simply reaching this point was so exhausting that I stopped for the night.

That Sickening Color of Yellow

The following night I began again. This time Robert's house disappeared, and a new scene quickly revealed itself. Now a long filthy-dirty, yellow-colored barracks-like building became visible. The long building wing seemed perched on cinder blocks roughly 2-3 feet off the ground. There was a stench that came from this building, a disgusting smell; the bottom of the building seemed to be dripping – something. I could not tell what it was but the thick, sticky almost oozing droplets seemed to be random.

The 100-foot-long building had windows on both sides with no screens. There were other buildings in more square shapes nearby. A border of dirt surrounded each building and then acres of haphazard wrinkled chicken wire in all directions lay on top of the ground. I also got a sense of odd black clouds hovering in many places here.

Ghost Stories from the Ghosts' Point of View

A sickening sense of nausea began to envelope me, a dread of knowing what I was about to find. Finally, I knew.

This hideous yellow barracks building was a Civil War clinic run by the Union Army to treat Confederate prisoners of war. That awareness was simply given to me. I have no idea how else to describe it. 'Knowingness' came over me with a deep grief that is difficult to articulate: I just knew.

The clinic was hurriedly constructed toward the end of the Civil War. By then, medical supplies were seriously dwindling. The only type of anesthetic used during that time was ether and there was seldom enough of this, much less pain medication to ease their suffering. Doctors were left with no useable supplies to treat tortured men. What little was available went to the Northern casualties.

Now I have the unenviable job of walking the hallways of the tortured and dying. I come upon a filthy, stinking surgery ward. There are primitive wooden tables where the surgeries were performed. These doctors were more like butchers than physicians dedicated to the preservation of life. The shock of catastrophic operations and thousands of amputations, performed without the benefit or compassion of any anesthetic would scar the living, as well as those who died.

How did they do it? How could these

surgeons heap such tremendous pain and indignity on their patients day after day? Did they become hardened to it? Did it affect them? How were they able to operate knowing the unintentional and unimaginable torture they put these men through? Did the screams of these helpless injured men haunt these surgeons for lifetimes to come?

The blood that pooled on the floor ran out holes drilled into the floorboards so that the earth below would soak up the life force of men too young to die or who were forever maimed.

For those poor souls who actually survived the butchery of the surgery, there were 'recovery' rooms where the patients were kept after their operations. None of these men were given any pain medication. These post-surgery rooms also had holes in the floorboards so that the blood and the yellow pus of infection would drip to the ground and reduce maintenance. Many soldiers never left that ward, so many had catastrophic injuries or were amputees who bled to death because there were no blood-clotting drugs at that time.

I dared not even imagine how the surgeons, nurses and orderlies could bear to hear the anguish of the cries, the whimpers, the retching of the men who often screamed themselves to death in hopes of escaping the pain of their mutilated bodies. The medical staff did not care what side these men had fought on, only that, as human beings, they deserved better than this perpetual torment, better than what they had to give them.

Imagine the personal agony for the physicians in such an untenable, horrific situation. They were dedicated to healing, the perpetuation of life, not the infliction and perpetuation of pain. Antibiotics were not invented until 1928 and were not available until the 1940s, so there was no way to stop infections. Nursing staff would have been the few women, who had no formal training, who volunteered from nearby farms. There was little food to nourish anyone. It was hell on earth for both the staff and the injured prisoners.

Flies covered the men and gathered like black cloud swarms on the earth below the barracks as well on the infections of men in the recovery wards. The stench of rotting flesh and yellow oozing infections was gagging in this hospital. There was no sanitation: instruments were never sanitized between patients; the wards were never cleaned, and doctors never washed their hands between operations. There were no clean linens, or unsoiled bandages. The real miracle is that anyone survived this medical facility.

Ward of the Damned

I marshaled my courage and continued my view.

As I watched this new scene unfold, I had not anticipated that I would be able to smell the stench of the dying, rotting men lying in those wards. A quick merciful end would have surely been preferable for many of them, rather than the agonizing hell of lonely, excruciatingly painful deaths. The medical staff moved around each suffering soul in their deeply blood-stained clothes, emotionless. Their mechanical movements made them appear to be numb to the misery before them.

But one doctor caught my eye. He seemed to be suffering emotionally with his dying charges, as if he had not turned off his heart, had not become immune to the sorrow before him.

I watched him speak to each man, acknowledge him, and ask him how he was feeling.

This doctor touched each patient with a tender hand on a forehand, a gentle squeeze of a man's hand or a pat on the shoulder of a sobbing soldier.

He listened to their barely audible whispered pleas to let their families know what happened to them after they died.

As he stayed by the side of one hideously

wounded man, he prayed with him and as this soldier took his last breath, this doctor looked up and asked God to take that man's soul. He tenderly closed the soldier's eyes and as the doctor turned away, as the tears ran down his face, I could see that this physician was my client, Robert. He was the commanding officer of this Union Army hospital clinic. He was in charge and this staggering responsibility weighted him down to his very core.

Yet the compassion that he shared with each patient never wavered, was never wanting. He cared about each man to the depth of his own soul, grieving them all with what little energy he had left.

Confederate Territory

I watched him walk the red stained, creaking floors of his 'command.' This medical structure was called a 'clinic' because then the Army would not have to fully fund or supply it. True hospitals were afforded more supplies. Having a clinic in Confederate territory made his job that much harder because he was living among his enemies and trying to help enemy soldiers. Robert felt as tormented as the patients. He, a Union Army Colonel, was left to beg for supplies from nearby farmers, praying for the kindness of strangers to help Confederate soldiers, but the neighboring farms had already been stripped. There was nothing left. Farmers were starving to death themselves.

There was another dwelling nearby, where doctors, nurses and orderlies slept. They could hear the screams of dying men all night long. Most of these physicians cried every night for the torture they inflected on their patients. The robotic façade falling away as the flood of emotion engulfed each one. The memories of those soldiers in prolonged agony stayed with them until their own deaths took them many decades later.

As I watched this scene, I began to wonder if these memories were what was still haunting people who had reincarnated in this current life. The Civil War was barely 140 years ago. Perhaps this scene, this subtle memory, was what was really haunting Robert.

Acres of Chicken Wire

The carnage of cannon ball blasts, rifle shots, and the staggering butchery of hand-to-hand combat left men with jagged wounds and non-functioning slowly rotting body parts.

The echoes of the screaming men, pleading, begging surgeons not to sever their limbs filled the halls of the clinic and overwhelmed Robert's heart. Amputation surgeries were performed daily – with no anesthetic. Men were told to "bite down real hard on this here piece of wood. . ." If they were lucky, they passed out from the pain and shock. Each man who survived the surgery immediately grieved his missing body part trying to imagine how he could make a living without one or both legs, or the loss of an arm or hand. Laying in the recovery rooms, these anguished souls could see the chicken wire out the window. At first, they had no idea what that was for but soon, soon they found out.

Body parts accumulated in jumbled piles in bloody buckets. Severed legs, hands, feet, and fingers were sticking up like some ghoulish abstract collection. The body parts from these daily amputations could not be burned because of the stench of burning human flesh. Instead, they were buried in the nearby fields. Trees had been cut down to make room for more buildings that were never built. When the body parts accumulated, soldiers were sent out to bury them in these nearby open fields. Now, with a sickening sense, I understand the purpose of the chicken wire. Rolls of chicken wire were placed over burial areas so that animals would not dig them up. The stench of rotting flesh was so horrible that it gagged the soldiers who had to dig the new amputation burial pits every day.

Life After the Civil War

Roughly 1000 men died in this hospital, in this blister dimension of hell. There were so many causalities by the end of the Civil War that at some point, the doctors simply dropped from exhaustion.

The entire building was burned to the ground at the end of the war. All of the bones of all of the limbs were dug up from under the chicken wire and dumped at sea. In its place, trees were planted in a desperate attempt to heal the earth.

The names of the dead men were sent back, if possible, to their homes, but so many plantations and farms were destroyed in the 4,000 Civil War battles, that notifications often went unread. Mass graves were used at this hospital due to the sheer volume of dead and the lack of embalming facilities. Tragically, most of these men had no identification, no names. Eventually, they became anonymous men and boys slaughtered: the Unknown Soldiers.

Incredibly, in that previous life, Robert lived through this Civil War hell. He had fought the Army bureaucracy for better health care for all military people regardless of the side that created their injury. Rebel or Yankee, it mattered not to him and his staff. All the faces looked alike and the injuries were gut wrenching for all in this sickening performance of man's inhumanity to man.

Robert still heals people in his current life as a physician, but he does not have the stomach to be a surgeon in this lifetime. One lifetime as a surgeon was enough for him. I believe that the high blood pressure he experiences in this life is the accumulated rage at the senseless deaths and torture experienced by those men in that past life.

And Then the Forsaken Appeared

I knew I was being watched. I could feel them as I went about my task of spiritually dismantling and clearing all the buildings of the energy of pain and death on this property. Restorative energy was lovingly applied to the land to relieve the abuse and misery that the earth had absorbed from every drop of blood and infection, every buried limb, and each hastily buried body. The earth suffers dearly as the life force of so many seeps into the ground. Sadness drapes the land like black funeral crepe flowing in waves across the earth. This noxious energy was carefully removed.

And I knew they watched this happen and I knew they could feel that subtle sigh of relief that the earth experienced with the return of the energies of blessing and hope.

Once this initial healing application was complete, they suddenly appeared almost as if a fog had cleared and they were standing there, thousands of them. I knew they would come, that it was merely a matter of time before I would see them, but that knowledge did not stop my dread as they began to speak to me.

"Ma'am, can you make the pain stop?" asked a soldier with his intestines dangling sickeningly from his abdomen.

"Can you help me find my mamma? I miss her so much." The request from this child/soldier of fourteen made me turn away as part of his face was simply gone.

"I can't find my legs. (Now screaming) I can't find my legs!"

"My hand got shot off, I have to tell my First Sergeant. He'll want to know 'cause I can't shoot Yankees no more." He made this statement woodenly as if the shock of losing his hand had not penetrated his consciousness.

"What am I doing here? I think I'm fine? Am I okay?" This soldier had not a mark on his fully intact body, but his uniform was studded in black soot, and I could only speculate that the shock wave of a cannon blast killed him instantly.

"Ma'am, I'm so tired, I ain't got no energy, can you help me?" I inwardly shuddered looking at the deep knife wound that opened up his heart allowing his life force to seep down his leg in a steady red stream.

Their war weary faces bespoke the truth: they were all at the end of their endurance, ready to go home. Military men everyone, they needed a return to a modest order of discipline – and compassion.

"Attention! Soldiers, good news, you're all finally going home. Time to assemble. Please line up. A blanket is being issued to each of you. Your orders are to join the escorts provided, to cross that bridge over there. If you cannot walk, your escort will help you make this crossing. Once you have crossed over, your questions will be answered, and your pain relieved. It's time to go men, your families are waiting and are anxious to welcome you home!"

I readied the healing blankets in neat piles so that each military man could take his spiritual turn at receiving healing and hope. The angels helped to wrap each man in his blanket, and then tenderly lifted each soldier and carried him into the light. Each maimed, crippled, mutilated and mortally wounded man could instantly feel the warmth of heaven embrace his battered body.

I stood as silent witness as one by one each soldier looked into the loving eyes of his angel. His body finally relaxed, arms limp by his side.

Some of them cried, deep exhausted sobs. Some of them smiled for the first time in a very long time. Some, in a moment of serene tenderness, reached up and touched the face of their angels and tears of relief and joy streamed down their grimy faces when their touch was rewarded by a glowing smile. Restoration began immediately with the touch of their heavenly companions: limbs were restored, wounds vanished, blood disappeared, and each man was rendered clean and whole as he crossed that bridge to the light.

In those private moments during the war, when each man tried to quell the overwhelming homesickness for wives, mothers, fathers, siblings, and children, he would have imagined again and again what that reunion with them would be like. And now that it was actually happening, now that their longing was over, there was an explosion of joy. Family members met each other with tearful hugs and kisses, and longing looks into their welcoming faces, each thrilled to realize that their beloved was finally home.

Even though these thousands of men may have died alone, unknown and in agony, at least now, in this precious moment, they were experiencing that sense of renewal that can only come from the joy of reunion and healing, found only in the Heaven World.

Epilogue

Once all of these men had been assisted to the Heaven World, I worked diligently to finish cleaning the earth, clearing the property of this dark energy of pain and sadness and bring light, hope and healing to this spot of land. The earth is alive, is a living being; the abuse the earth suffers in any violent conflict is tremendous and requires healing.

Robert's desire to learn improved therapeutic techniques stemmed from this time when he lacked the tools to save those men. His heart is still with them, and for the ones who died and lingered, he has now given them the best healing he could possibly have provided: release . . . home to God. It was not his fault so many died. He truly did the very best that he could.

I checked on the property a third night and it finally felt at peace. Robert said that he was also at peace, that he felt better somehow. I explained to him that the work on the clinic had taken place on a particular piece of property, not necessarily his current home property. I do not know where this Civil War hospital actually was but through the connection that Robert had with it in that previous stack of time, I was able to provide clearing and healing to the land as well as a release for all of those horribly tortured souls. As I was explaining what happened at that hospital, Robert commented that he was probably one of the doctors there. Odd that he never considered himself one of the soldiers – somehow, he just knew.

Through an unusual chain of events, I was made aware of a book put out by the Union Army with a history of the Civil War doctors who served during that war. There was Robert's picture. He looks the same today as he did then. He came back, reincarnated again to help people. His mission was to heal those men and although he could not do that in that time, he has now finally completed his mission. He is still personally recovering from the horror of that most recent past life. Perhaps someday he too, can heal. I sincerely hope so.

The Brazilian Jeweler

Jewelry Shopping in Brazil

I love Brazil! This country has the most gorgeous stones: amethyst, blue topaz, aquamarine, Rubellite tourmaline, golden and imperial topaz, Brazilian emeralds, red and green tourmaline and the stunning teal of the newly discovered stone, Paraiba.

My husband was in Rio for a conference, so we came a bit early and had a glorious week in Rio de Janeiro in a hotel overlooking the colorful umbrella-dotted, Copacabana Beach.

My favorite past time is shopping, looking for all kinds of jewels. Prices in the big-name jewelry houses were super high, so we decided to walk the back streets by the hotel to find smaller neighborhood jewelry stores. This is where the locals shop. We were not disappointed.

Twinkling Jewels and the Paranormal

Right away, we found a jewelry store run by a lovely couple, who had been in this business for years. I was looking for pretty treasures for my sister, my niece, my daughter and my two daughters-in-law. The jeweler welcomed us in, offered us that wonderful, rich, full-bodied Brazilian coffee, as we sat down to talk stones.

Her name was Monique and she had dazzling both loose and set jewels. We chatted about why Troy and I were in Brazil and that I was looking for pretty treasures for my family. She herself had a daughter who now lived in Israel. She told me she was about to ship loose amethyst stones to her daughter's shop and asked if I would like to see them.

When you work with a jeweler, pleasantries are important. You have to get to know each other. She asked me what stones I was interested in and for whom.

But before I could answer her, I began to cough, that telltale psychic cough that feels like I am breathing in black smoke. This dry cough tells me something negative or dead is present.

Monique offered me a glass of water to help with the coughing. And then she proceeded to show me a beautiful collection of all types of precious stones. Between coughing spells, I was able to communicate that we were the most interested in amethyst. The coughing continued while Monique left the room to find her exceptional collection of cut amethyst stones on their way to Israel.

She returned with several white folded paper packages with writing on the outside indicating the size and type of lose stones tucked inside. The amethysts were so gorgeous they took my breath away. But I was unable to fully enjoy them because I was coughing so hard.

"Please help us! She won't let us go! She's holding us so tightly that we cannot seem to leave here. Please tell her to let us go!"

I was unable to tell the age or relationship to Monique of this male presence begging me to ask Monique to release him and someone else. It was hard to hear this ghost because the amethysts, topaz, emeralds, and rubies surrounding me in the display cases were so stunningly distracting or maybe the reverse was true: possibly the stones actually facilitated ghostly communications.

Letting Go

"I'll try, but I don't know Monique that well." I told this Brazilian ghost through the vehicle that is mental telepathy on the psychic realm.

"You must help us. She has a tremendous

hold on us. If you leave, she won't let us go."

"I can't force her to release you. I'll do what I can." I assured him.

I knew I had to say something to Monique. Now, this is a hard decision. I've known this woman for a mere ten minutes. Saying anything to her about the paranormal is going to be bizarre, beyond strange. But I was getting a sense that there was more than one ghost standing behind her and they were not giving up pressuring me to help them.

As Monique was dazzling me with these deep, violet, amethysts that were bursting with crimson light and fire, I broached the subject.

"I hate to be so personal, but I'm getting an exceptionally strong feeling that there is someone with you, several people, actually, standing behind you. Have you had anyone close to you pass away recently? This could be someone you're still grieving perhaps?"

Monique blinked. My husband rolled his eyes, shifted uncomfortably in his seat next to me and tried to pretend he didn't really know me. Even after 39 years together, these kinds of situations are still hard for him.

Monique never turned a hair.

"No one has died recently at all."

I persisted that someone was with her.

"Oh, I know, it's my parents. They died several years ago. They're with me still."

"Have you considered helping them to

cross over? Are you ready to let them go?" I was hoping she would show some emotion, some element of a willingness to help her parents to leave. The amethysts twinkled brightly between us. My coughing had ceased, almost as if someone had turned off a switch, telling me I was on the right track.

"No. I love keeping them with me. They've been with me for years and I can feel them all the time. Should I release them?" She pondered this concept for a few seconds.

"Oh yes, it would be so good for them to finally be able to cross over. They would appreciate this help so much." I said this hopefully. I was optimistic that by opening this door I could get her to let them go. The fact that they made their presence known to me so insistently indicated that they wanted to be released from that 4th dimensional world.

"Well, I'm not ready to release them. I need to keep them with me, to keep them safe here by me. I would miss them too much if I released them." She made this statement without emotion, almost as if she had thought about it before and decided against releasing her ghostly parents.

I'm sure she did not realize that her seemingly loving desire to have her parents with her for eternity was ultimately not in her parents' best interest. She could not conceive of their need to leave her, and she also could not imagine life without their presence.

The conversation felt over. She was handling her grief by holding on to her parents so tightly that they could never leave. I could not force her to release her attachment to her dead parents.

Deep Violet Amethysts

We returned to opening those innocuous looking, plain white packages. Each held two or three deep Lilac amethysts. Some stones were so large they needed their own zip code. One stunner was a whopping thirty karats, just under the size of a tablespoon measure. This stone's color was so powerful that when I held it up to the light, I could see flashes of red dancing inside the facets.

"Monique, these stones are unlike any amethysts I have ever seen. I can't take my hands off of them. Each one I hold feels alive with power and energy. I'm looking for a beautiful stone for a ring."

"You won't be able to lift your hand if you buy that huge one." My husband decided to pull me back to reality. Monique smiled at Troy and quickly helped direct me back to less weighty gems.

"No problem. Let's look at a few smaller ones, in the 15-karat range. See, these are equally filled with fire."

I turned my attention back to the stones. Monique was able to show me smaller stones that still danced with life and begged to go home with me. Maybe it was the energy of the stones or the disappointment of the ghosts that caused this wave of weariness to come over me, but I knew I had to leave.

I thanked Monique and told her I had to think about what I had seen, and we left. My hope was that she would think about what I had told her, as well about her parents. Maybe she would now consider releasing them.

"She's never going to release us, is she . . ." Her father made this statement with profound disappointment.

"No, at least not now. She may change her mind in the future, and we have to give her a chance to think about it. I've done what I can, but I can't force her. I have to go on the premise that no energy is ever wasted and that our brief encounter will perhaps enable Monique to eventually release you."

I never fail to be amazed by how readily someone will admit to holding on to his or her loved ones. I can see what looks like black cords that imprison these souls, emanating from the living person's solar plexus extending in choking cords wrapped around the ghost's very soul. It starts out slowly and begins to build and build over time until the soul cannot set itself free. No one can fully heal their own grief until they have completely cut those cords and finally allowed their loved one(s), to heal by crossing into the light. When this happens, then healing for the entire family can be facilitated.

A Stunning Purchase

I did eventually buy one of the smaller (not the 30-karat size) amethyst stones from Monique and her husband the next day and the stone became a stunning custom-made ring. When my husband and I went to pick up the ring three days later, we spoke to Monique and her husband again. She did not speak of her parents, but we are now connected through the magic of this exquisite amethyst and our aka cords. Who knows how it will all work out? Perhaps the 'magic' of the stones will help those trapped souls after all. Little did I know that karma and circumstance would eventually rule the day.

Fortune smiled upon me in 2013 and once again I was able to join my handsome husband in Rio for another conference. Not long after we were settled in our hotel, we revisited the many lovely places we had enjoyed the previous year.

We again found ourselves on the back streets off of Copacabana Beach and wandered back to that wonderful jeweler. This time, Monique was in Israel with their daughter and granddaughter. But her parents were still in the store. I was surprised to realize that they were more chained to the store than to Monique. I had no explanation for this.

Monique's husband was there and before we spoke to him, we waited while he was helping other customers. It was then that Monique's parents approached me.

"We won't ever leave here without your help. She holds us here in the store, as if we are tethered to her somehow. Please understand, we love her, we do, but we want to be free of this tiring existence. Please help us to cross over."

"This shop is not my property, so I have no jurisdiction here. If you were both to follow me out to the sidewalk, to a public area, then I can help you immediately because I have spiritual jurisdiction."

"We're not sure. We are tied to the store. It's so hard."

"You may be tired to the store, but even in the 4th dimension, you still have the power of free will. Tethered or not, you have the spiritual free will to walk the few steps to join me outside on the sidewalk where I can help you cross over. I am also providing both of you the comfort of these two angels. You can ask them for help at any moment to cross you both over, even here in the store and it will be done. Just ask and those dark ties that bind you in that timeless, space-less void, will vanish instantly as you begin your immediate transition to the Heaven World. Your daughter will still be all right and you can communicate with her in a spiritually correct way from the Heaven World. You must choose."

I do not know what choices those ghosts made. I have done all that I can. All any of us can do is follow spiritual law, do our best and hope that souls choose the light whenever it is possible to do so. I will not be returning to Brazil; that time is over as well as any future contact with these souls. I pray that they will find that light bridge to the Heaven World.

Reverend Rutherford

Looking down on the address in coastal Virginia, I see a neighborhood subdivision of neat houses in typically ordered rows. Everyone has a green back yard, some type of fence, grass, a tree here and there, the obligatory grill for the manly cooks among us, a backyard swing, a doghouse. Front yards look similar with azaleas, Sycamore trees, the glorious yellow of forsythia, and a fruit tree scattered here and there. Cars are parked out front. An apartment building is nearby. A strip mall is not far away. It is all very civilized, boring, orderly, and seemingly safe and secure. The only sparse clump of trees is perhaps in a park a half mile or so away.

When you look at it all from above, you cannot seem to conceive of what might have happened in that manicured spot in another time, in that exact same space.

That exact space is home to stacks of time. How many lives ago could it have been, when other people lived on that very spot and had experiences, struggles and tragedies? Few locations on the Earth are without predecessor energy, the energy of those people, animals and life events that have come before us. Life is a never-ending story. We simply drop into the drama of our parents' lives at the moment we are born and never think about what or who came before us.

But others came before us. They lived and died often on the very spot where we are living. Those ghosts can influence us, whether we are aware of them or not.

So, I received a request to look at a rental house in this neat, modern neighborhood that the owners think is haunted. They have renters and their renters are always having violent fights. The landlord shared that he felt that the problems had become chronic. He knew something had to be done. He described the domestic and child abuse as unending. Police seem to intervene at this address frequently. Things were always breaking down in the house. (I sensed that there is the energy of rage and of fire based on what he said.) Finally, the landlord decided that maybe there was something else influencing that plot of ground. He called and asked if I would take a look and let him know if I found anything.

Slipping Through Time and Space

When I remote view any location, I close my eyes, memorize the location, and begin to consciously project my consciousness to a specific address once I have the owner's permission. I'm not asleep, but 'awake' in another place, fully aware of where I am. I find myself standing there at the precise position given. At first, I see what is currently there: the house, the car in the driveway, trees, and the front door. Then I enter the house; I enter the etheric house. This means that I find myself inside the dwelling looking at what is etherically there, not necessarily physically there. People are often concerned that I will see how messy their house is, or that there are areas they forgot to dust. I cannot see that. It's not what I am looking for in that space.

I set my intention to be shown that event, person, situation, or natural disaster, which is currently influencing the energy of this spot on the earth.

I am patient.

Time passes.

As I move around the house, I notice that it begins to shift to another time and space. The scene finally shifts to utter darkness and then wispy mists.

More time passes and then suddenly I see

it, I have stepped into the middle of an event unfolding right before my eyes. I also get a feeling for which stack of time I have entered. My sense was that this stack was 1679.

Sweet Marie and Michelle

I immediately see two beautifully and expensively dressed little girls with long, curly blond hair in matching dark blue tweed coats. I watched, mesmerized, as these two gorgeous children raced through the thick woods. It's dusk now and it will be dark soon. I cannot imagine that either of them can see where they are going. Their leggings are scratched, and their legs are bleeding. Both of them are utterly terrified as they continue frantically looking behind them, as if they are sure someone is following them. I can feel the cold gnawing of their fear, as if someone had filled me with that same sickening panic. They are holding hands, breathless as they eternally seek to outrun some unseen evil, as if the devil himself were chasing them.

At some point, both girls seemed to be able to see me and I gently attempted to speak with them. They stopped, gasping for breath, furtively glancing behind them, waiting for some inevitable terror to grab them at any second.

"Girls, can you see me?" I ventured.

"Yes, but you have to run with us, or he'll catch us! Hurry! Run!" She screamed at me as if she had to protect us all.

"Girls, I'm here to protect you. Stop. You don't have to run anymore. Can you tell me your names please?"

The girls looked nervously around them, unsure, untrusting.

"I'm Michelle. This is Marie."

I guessed at their ages. I figured Marie to be about 4 and a half and Michelle seemed around 7 years old. There were no obvious marks on them save their scratched legs, but they were terrified as if something or someone was about to do them great harm.

"Girls, can you tell me why you're so terrified? What are you running from? Where are your parents?"

The girls exchanged nervous glances and Michelle began to share what she perceived happened.

"We, uh, we came from France with maman and papa. The ship ride across the sea was bad. We were sick a lot. We kept hearing our parents talk about the New World, that it was a special chance to start a new life, with a new adventure. I didn't understand why we had to leave our beautiful home in France. I loved it there. We miss our dolls so much. But we are here. We had church friends and maman said they sponsored us. I don't know what that means."

I knew she was speaking French, but there is no language barrier in the ether. It does not matter what language someone speaks once he or she has died. It is all understandable to the psychic, without need for translation because the energy of communication is universal in the 4th dimension.

"Michelle, what happened when you arrived?"

"Reverend Rutherford wrote to our parents while we were living in France. He said his church would sponsor us. I don't know what 'sponsor' means. All I know is that after we got that letter maman and papa told us to get ready to go to 'the new world.'

"The Reverend, he met the ship when we arrived in Virginia. I remember that I had never seen so many trees as they have here. Other church people welcomed us to their homes, and we stayed with them."

Then Marie interrupted.

"But we don't speak any English. Maman and papa wanted us to learn English. Reverend Rutherford said that his wife spoke French and she could teach us English."

"Oh, so you girls met the Reverend's wife when she greeted the boat?"

"No," Michelle continued. "No, we never got to see her. The Reverend said that she was very shy but that she loved children. He said that he had a place not far from here with room for us to stay with them for a while and learn English. When I heard him say this, I felt – I felt . . . We didn't want to leave maman and papa." Then Marie continued.

"I didn't like Reverend Rutherford. I was afraid when I looked at him, and I tried to tell maman, but she didn't listen. She said that he was a 'man of the cloth' and that I didn't need to be afraid. I don't know what that means. What kind of cloth? Whatever cloth he had; I didn't like him." Marie felt strongly that she wanted me to know that she didn't like Reverend Rutherford at any point.

Parents often dismiss a child's concern about a person. Marie's fears of the Reverend might have been embarrassing for the parents since they were indebted to him for sponsoring the entire family and arranging families where they could stay upon arrival. But children see things with different eyes; they saw the true color of Reverend Rutherford's cloth. Michelle continued.

"Reverend Rutherford said he didn't have room for our parents to stay with us at his cottage, so our parents agreed to let us go by ourselves with him. We didn't want to go."

Both girls stared at the ground. They stopped talking, remembering, with a cold shudder, why they were running, why they did not trust this 'man of the cloth.' I felt myself involuntarily shiver as well.

Michelle continued.

"Everything was different here. Food tasted funny. People wore very different clothes, like they were so poor. Marie and I were afraid all the time. Nothing was familiar.

"We had only been here for a week when maman and papa handed us over to Reverend Rutherford. We were so afraid because we didn't know the woods. There were so many trees. We were so terrified of him. He took us firmly by our hands and . . . and, then Marie started to cry. She cried all the way to his house. Our parents should have gone with us. Why didn't papa come with us? Why did maman trust this bad man? Maman looked at us and I saw fear on her face, but papa said that we would be fine. He shouted that he would be by to pick us up in a few days. Smile, he said, soon you will know English. That was the last French we ever heard.

"I didn't want to learn English. Reverend Rutherford didn't speak French. We didn't know what he was saying to us. He didn't smile anymore after maman and papa were out of sight. He dragged us by our hands so fast we could not keep up with him. His nice manner vanished when we left our parents. His house was not 'nearby,' it was a long, long walk. We didn't recognize anything. All the trees looked the same."

As Michelle was lamenting this journey, I realized that this was how their legs came to be scratched and bleeding.

The Reverend's Wife

"What happened when you got to his house? Was his wife there?"

"No, we never saw any sign of his wife - ever." Michelle said emphatically.

"We got to his house, and he let go of our hands and we ran to each other and hugged really close. We tried to ask him where his wife was, but he didn't speak French. He laughed in a mean way. I tried to understand him, but I couldn't. I guess that's when we knew we had to get out of his house. That's when we broke free and ran into these woods and started running."

"Michelle, did you see any evidence that he even had a wife?"

"Yes, it looked like a woman had been there, but the house felt cold, like it was a bad place. We never saw her. I wonder if he killed her. We're just glad we got out of that scary house. We've been running in these woods ever since. He hasn't caught us yet. Maybe we can run back to our parents. We keep getting lost. We're so cold. Light Lady, we're tired, and confused. Can you help us find maman and papa? We want to return to Paris, to our friends, to people who speak French, where food tastes good and we're safe. This is a very, very bad man! We think that if we had stayed there, he - he would have killed us . . . like we think he killed his wife." Michelle was ever hopeful that they were going to be reunited with their parents.

It never occurred to either child that they were both already dead. They would never be reunited with their parents in life, speak French again, or get to grow up.

As they were speaking, I quietly brought in children angels to share this space so that they would no longer feel so cold, or alone, and I laid out food and blankets. Finally, I asked the angels to bring in dolls for each bewildered child.

"Girls, come join these other little girls in this lovely circle. They are enjoying all this food and there are cozy quilts for you both. There are even dolls that need love here. Just come and rest here a while. I'll keep you safe."

Marie was unsure. "How can this be here? Is this safe, Michelle?"

"It feels happy in that circle. We'll stop just for a little while, then we'll get this nice Light Lady to help us find our parents." I had the feeling that Michelle was beginning to understand what was happening.

The Man of the Bloody Cloth

Despite what the girls think happened, I suspect that their subconscious simply shut down and created a different reality from what they actually experienced. I can completely understand why. While the girls were with the angels, a very different, extremely vicious story unfolded for me to see.

When the girls got into the house and saw no trace of Reverend Rutherford's wife, they became terrified. He made no pretense to be kind to them. He literally dragged them through the woods. I suspect that the girls were too terrified to scream. Somehow a survival instinct took over and they made plans to escape even though they did not know the area. It was already becoming dark and they were hungry.

Reverend Rutherford, that devil in a minister's frock, did not even try to put them at ease. He immediately tied up Michelle and began to attack and rape Marie. The horror for Michelle, unable to protect and defend her younger sister, must have been an unspeakable torture. She could see wide-eyed little Marie screaming for her life. Combine this with the fact that Michelle knew with that certain agony of inevitability that her turn was next. This man appeared to be the devil himself to these girls. He raped each girl with a ghastly delight, while she was alive and screaming. Then he strangled each innocent child to death.

The girls think they have escaped this evil man. But what really happened was that they both left their bodies and ran outside – what they thought was outside but what in reality was simply the ether. They became stuck in the valley of the shadow of death – the 4th dimension where they have been running through the dark, chilly, forbidding woods for over 340 years. They are eternally feeling the chill of death, the stabbing pain of betrayal and the abandonment of their parents.

Reverend Rutherford raped and murdered these girls just as he had his wife, and he buried them alongside his dead wife, beneath the floorboards of his house in the dirt so that dogs and wolves would not dig them up. His place was so cold. That must have been how he managed to evade the gruesome smell of decomposing bodies. Even people who came to look for them would not guess that their brutalized, battered bodies were lying inches beneath their feet as Reverend Rutherford cleverly explained away their absence.

Wrapping the Lie in Cloth

Reverend Rutherford explained the disappearance of his wife and the two girls by saying that they somehow all got lost in the woods. He claimed he turned his back and the girls ran out in search of their parents. He said he called for them, that he and his wife searched for them for hours but when it became dark, he gave up. His wife never returned from the search either. The children's parents were horrified. They could not understand how both this man's wife and their children could disappear in one night. They could also not understand why Reverend Rutherford did not immediately call for everyone to look for these three lost souls. However, this man was so intimidating, so formidable that people hesitated to question him. He was a minister, a man of the cloth, seemingly above reproach.

The French mother remembered the terrified look on the faces of her girls when they were taken to his home. I would imagine that this last guilt-laden visual memory of her girls haunted her until her own death. Both parents eventually returned to France after no search party could ever turn up even a trace of either child much less the Reverend's wife.

Reverend Rutherford had been held in high regard. However, this small close-knit community was becoming increasingly suspicious of him. People remembered that his wife and these poor French children vanished, and then other children disappeared. In each case he was the last one to see them all alive.

The term 'serial killer' and 'pedophile' would have been unheard of in that time. This small tight knit community would have had no way to adequately explain the terrible uneasy feeling they had about him. Without direct evidence, they could not confront him. But their suspicions deepened when this coldly intimidating man seemed to have one strange and bizarre event after the other happen to and around him. Two years after the French girls vanished, his shack inexplicably burned to the ground: he burned to death in that conflagration. He always elicited more questions about his life and death than answers could be found. Why was he unable to escape his burning home? What happened to him? Why did only his house burn and not the surrounding forest?

Colonists sifting through the ashes discovered his body and the bodies of his victims.

No one grieved him.

His house was leveled, and no one wanted that property. Nothing was built on this tragic plot of land for a very long time.

The Healing of Reunion

Finally, with both girls in the healing circle,

they were feeling much warmer, both physically and emotionally. It is hard to fathom how a ghost can feel cold, but perhaps understanding that the cold they seem to feel is an 'emotional chill' that transcends time and space. When someone is guilty or terrified, there is a sense of being cold that will penetrate the person to the very depth of his or her soul.

Once the crossing over bridge is opened, the warmth and the welcoming light are tremendously attractive to souls that need this compassion, which is why I was unable to see them at first. Only Marie and Michelle were with me initially; then slowly the other children who had been the tragic victims of Reverend Rutherford appeared. Then other children who died by other means appeared as well as other colonists who had died a variety of ways. All were welcome in this well of light.

Angels located the parents of all the children Reverend Rutherford had murdered so that they could all finally be reunited. In the electrifying instant when the parents were reunited with their children, the energy of the past slipped away and all that remained was the explosive joy of love. Parents bent down and lifted their sweet ones up, hugged them, and covered them with kisses. Happy tears freely streamed down everyone's faces. The longing was gone. A tremendous amount of healing took place in that one remarkable moment for both parents and children. The loss of a child engenders such profound grief for any parent and sometimes guilt at the method of the child's death or disappearance. Such a reunion instantly begins the healing process for the parents.

Then the angels signaled that they were ready for the crossover. The children took the hands of their parents and the angels and as they all approached the crossing-over point, they were able to see the glorious light of the Divine.

Marie and Michelle watched wistfully as all of those other children were reunited with their parents. They looked at me with that glimmer of hope that means that just maybe someone wonderful would be there for them. And they were. Their own parents had also been in a hell of self-imposed guilt because they let their children out of their sight. They believed that they alone were responsible for their children's death, for trusting Reverend Rutherford. It is a feeling that anyone can understand: missing children are an unending nightmare for any parent.

I suspected that the parents of Marie and Michelle would have been seeking their children, even in death. Guilt will prevent many a good soul from embracing the light of the crossing over point.

"Marie, Michelle, I want you to look right over there. Do you see your parents? Can you see your maman and papa? They're standing with those beautiful angels." Michelle hesitated, wanting to believe that their ordeal was over, yet cautious.

"We do. Can . . . can this be real? Have maman and papa come for us? This isn't a trick? We're so tired, we . . . we want to go home with our parents. Light Lady, is it okay now? Can we go home now?"

"Yes sweetheart, it's time to go home. Your parents are waiting with their angels. It's safe. See, I've brought in angels for both of you and they are going to escort you and your parents over this beautiful golden bridge. It's all right honey. It's time to go."

I took a deep breath, a breath of holding on to my own emotions. Both girls were slightly tentative at taking their first steps into the light. Then the glorious reality of that amazing glow embraced them. Finally, with their own angels in tow, they raced toward that light bridge as both of their parents came down on bended to knees to embrace each child. The golden light of the angels glowed ever so much brighter as they stood as silent witness to the love between parents and children that transcends death. The complete and utter joy of these reunions surely lit up heaven itself. Then they all made the crossover into the light.

I never knew the name of the Reverend's wife, but she did eventually come to find that peace of release from her own murder.

However, as the angels guided her into the Heaven World, the private agony she had experienced, watching her deviously pious husband torture and murder so many children, was released from her. She carried the guilt of being unable to stop him in time or to warn anyone of his murderous ways. But then, it was 1679 and women had no stature, so who would have believed her?

Reverend Rutherford finally appeared after the children and his wife had made their transition to the Heaven World. I could see him in a slightly separate stack of time because he died some time later. He always wore dark clothing, but this visual of him was charred black: his entire body was a burnt black mess. He did not speak to me.

"Rutherford, you will be escorted to that part of the Heaven World that handles vicious souls."

I wanted him to know that, while no soul is ever left behind, that he would be receiving different treatment. I also did not acknowledge his religious position. He only looked at me with a slight smile on his crisply burned lips. It was more of a sneer. Serial killers are psychopathic, sociopathic, narcissists. They never experience a moment of conscience in mortal life or death.

I brought in spiritual police to dispatch him to that appropriate realm, specifically reserved for those lethal souls to eventually work out the karma of mass murder.

Epilogue

It might be thought that the fire that killed Reverend Rutherford would purify the sight of so much violence. Many people believe that flames can purify any site in which there is fire. However, the fire could not purify the site because so many souls were trapped in that terrible place together even though they could not actually see each other, and none of them had been crossed over. It is always critically important to cross all souls over no matter when they died.

Clearing souls not only helps the individual souls, but it also helps the earth to rebalance, once the heavily toxic energy of ghosts is finally gone. Ghosts unknowingly add a spiritual 'weight' to a location and mortal people can feel this.

The property was cleaned and cleared. I suggested that the owner should plant evergreen trees there to further cleanse the land. Pine and/or fir trees are especially enhancing to any area constantly releasing negative ions into the air. Evergreen trees offer a softness to the landscape even in the coldest winters, offering the grace of the green of their needles.

Beautiful landscaping also helps to clean and clear an area with the bright flowers and steady influence of trees that helps to anchor a location in time and space in a happier place.

Eventually, the owner told me that the fighting among his tenants ceased and peace began to be felt throughout his property. Such is the result of this esoteric clearing and helping the dead to find the light of the Divine.

The Voiceless Souls of History

Old Colonial homes look beautiful, especially those elegant, gracious three and four story period structures on some of the South's most prestigious plantations. Some date to the early 1600s. These imposing buildings whisper hints of stories of settlers who came to build a country, when life was often grueling, and people struggled to make the raw, untapped riches of America part of everyday life.

When I stepped onto the grounds of the stately Berkeley Plantation in Charles City, Virginia, I immediately felt the energy of such a long-established home. What was lifelike in 1619 for these original 38 settlers who proclaimed, by official English Charter, this particular 8,000 acres by the James River, their land?

Plantations were erected on acreage

originally owned by no one, entirely part of nature. But once English settlers came to the lush lands that would eventually become the Carolinas, Virginia and the other colonies, land was owned, surveyed, and worked. These great estates produced products used throughout the original thirteen colonies and sold to England.

Berkeley Plantation is one of these classic Colonial American homes with multiple chimneys, handmade brick facades, creaking wood floors and manicured grounds. The current owners of this tremendous manor have preserved all of the 'out buildings' which included the blacksmith, stables, grain storage, the 'smokehouse' for curing meats and the housing for indentured servants and slaves. Even the kitchen was in another building where slaves and indentured servants prepared the food, carrying meals into the great house three times a day. The kitchen was always kept in a separate structure, to preclude the entire main house from burning down, in the event of a kitchen fire.

The daily challenge was intense: you grew, foraged, or hunted what you ate, wore, or used for construction. Managing a plantation, growing crops: corn, cotton, tobacco, indigo, alfalfa, flax, wheat, and the plantation vegetable garden was a backbreaking full-time job, one that took hundreds of hands to make profitable.

The survival of this plantation and its residents was never assured. Perseverance and love of this beautiful land were the tools that keep the landowners focused on building a life here. The challenges of that first fateful year must have been unimaginable. Perhaps this is why Berkeley Plantation became the site of the first official Thanksgiving ever held in America, on December 4, 1619. How grateful they must been to have survived their initial fateful year here.

By 1726, the large three-story house that is the heart of Berkeley Plantation today was erected. The original owners were Benjamin Harrison IV and his wife, Anne. When you visit this plantation today, you will see ten acres of formal boxwood gardens and the lush blanket of green that was and still is their front lawn, extending from the front door to the shores of the James River.

The Harrison family was critical to the founding of the United States. Benjamin Harrison V was a signer of the Declaration of Independence. William Henry Harrison was the 9th U.S. President and Berkeley Plantation was the ancestral home of Benjamin Harrison, the 23rd U.S. President. This particular plantation was also, for a time, the Headquarters and main supply base for McClellan's Union Army. When President

Abraham Lincoln reviewed the 140,000 Union troops, thereby approving their readiness for battle, he did it at Berkeley. And it was here, in 1862, that the haunting strings of notes for trumpet and bugle tones that came to be known as "Taps," was penned by Oliver W. Norton.

The names of the famous from the Harrison family are emblazoned on plaques, in history books and on the pages of the Declaration of Independence. However, the names of those who did not so willingly arrive here are long forgotten. These were the souls who landed here after making either a grudgingly arduous journey, or for some, being kidnapped, thrown aboard ship, and sold to the highest bidder. These were the voiceless souls of history. These were the indentured servants, and the slaves who made up the work force of the plantation. Indentured servants felt daunted by the challenge of making the land produce a living for the plantations. They tenaciously clung to the hope that they would survive the 7-10 years of their servitude and eventually build a life here. The African souls were disenfranchised from their homes, felt homesick without their own language, familiar food, and belief systems. Both groups struggled in this new world, of not only a radically different climate but also with often colliding sociological issues.

And it was while visiting this peaceful, verdant, Berkeley Planation, that I gained amazing insight into the world of these nameless, faceless, and ultimately voiceless souls. Although I was about to learn that many were no longer quite so silent about what their life – and death were like.

Visiting the Visitors

It was a beautiful spring day when I visited Berkeley Plantation with my family, and wandered the lawns, the grounds and found myself sitting in a charming screened-in gazebo of sorts on a far corner of the lawn. It felt comfortable in this pretty piece of history. Birds chirped in the stately trees nearby. Insects droned on and as I was sitting there, other sounds, other voices began to make their presence known.

I had not intended to slip through stacks of time, but as I closed my eyes to feel the essence of the plantation, I began to hear the voices of the past creep into my consciousness. It felt as if we, the visitors, were being visited by the residents, who lived and died on this patient stretch of land through many centuries past. I became very quiet, for to hear these still, soft voices often takes patience and the ability to tune out the present, to shut off the noise of the current time. And if you can do that, it's amazing what you can hear.

The First Americans

The first Americans, the Native Americans, spoke with intense sadness of the greed by which the English simply took what they believed to be theirs. I have no idea how many Native Americans were talking, only that their lament, their sense of tragedy was always the same. People simply landed on these shores and took over the land. The Native people had no idea what 'an acre of land' was. They had never heard of a person granting a 'Charter.' They could not imagine someone giving land that he or she had never even seen. They had no frame of reference for someone who arrogantly decided that he had dominion over these forests, and never once questioned if his actions were going to impact the people currently living there, the people who called this land their home.

Native people living along the Powhatan River (or the James River as the English called it) in Virginia were known as Powhatans or Algonquians. They were the first to make these forests their home, and they learned how to love and respect the land. The first English visitors were not invited by anyone. They were barely tolerated by the Native Americans. Their avaricious actions of taking land and demanding help made them hated. The English applied the term 'civilized society' only to other Englishman and some Europeans. They could not see that the first Americans were at one with the land. Nor could they conceive of how the Native people perceived their invaders.

Native peoples built structures that could be moved if the land became stressed, something that they could feel. No one owned anything. They simply used and moved, allowing the land to recover.

The longer the Powhatans observed the white man, the more baffled they became. These people barely knew how to survive. Had they initially not helped the English, those first settlements would have surely perished. However, more and more whites arrived and then, eventually, a new kind of human being was brought to the shores of Virginia: black men. The Powhatans were very wary of these new kinds of humans. Some thought these black-colored men, these Negroes as they were called, were evil because their eyes were black as well as their skin. Native American anxieties grew as time went on with the arrival of more and more Englishman and slaves. It was at this point, that a very tall black man in ragged clothing, who seemed insistent on sharing his story, approached me.

The Cruel Reality of African Confusion

"We didn't know what happened to us. We were trapped like animals in our village. Nets were thrown over us and we were beaten and dragged onto carts. One day I was chief of my tribe and the next I am in a place I do not understand, a place that smelled like death with blood, urine, and feces on the floor. Black men captured us, beat us, and sold us to white men. These traders made money on us.

"We never saw our families again. There were hundreds of men like me in these rooms with iron doors. There was little food, no light, and the fear we all felt clung to us like some suffocating wind. We didn't know what was happening to us since we couldn't understand anything that was said to us by white men.

"After several days in these rooms, we were washed with water and then chains were put around our ankles and wrists. Then we were marched to something I had never seen. It was a big wooden thing and it sat on the water. I had never seen that much water or a hut that big.

"When we walked up to it, I was afraid, we were all afraid, it was as if it was some kind of magic. Then we walked on to the moving hut. The hut moved all the time and we all started throwing up. They put us in a dark place. We did not recognize the food they gave us. Mostly we were so sick, that we could not eat the horrible food thrown in bowls in front of us. Many men died of starvation and throwing up."

"I don't know why I didn't die."

"I don't know why I didn't die. I didn't know what this thing, this big hut was that moved without end. No one spoke to us, told us what was happening to us, or where we were being taken and why."

This man is finally able to let someone know how he felt being forced into slavery. He shared the depth of his shock and grief at discovering that life as he knew it in Africa, was forever ended.

"Then one day, when I wished that I could die like so many others, the hut stopped moving so much and we heard voices, new voices I did not recognize.

"Someone came and opened a way for us to leave the moving hut. We walked down a piece of wood and stood, mostly naked, humiliated, and almost blind in the sunlight, on the land. We were skin and bones. Some men shook violently. Some vomited – again.

"It was cold here, so cold and we had no clothing. We were wearing what we had when we were captured. Someone offered us a blanket against the cold. I did not know if I should take it. We did not know why this happened to us, this journey of endless pain and sorrow.

"We stood in the bright light and as our eyes adjusted, we could see trees everywhere, like we had never seen before. But they were horrifying trees because there were men like us hanging in those trees, dead men with no clothes on, dead men – and we did not know why they were hung.

"No one spoke to us in any words we could understand.

"They took off our shackles and we could see how bloody our ankles were for the first time. One man tried to run away, and they hung him right there in front of us. Maybe it is easier to die than to live in a place that is so cold, no one knows your name, no one knows your words and death can come to you so quickly."

"Sold!"

"We stood there, men with no dignity left, reduced to quivering, shivering bodies of flesh without name, or land. I was placed on a tall piece of wood and there was talking, and I guessed they were talking about me. A white man in a brown hat and strange clothing pointed at me and raised his hand and I heard someone say 'Sold!' I didn't know what that meant.

"The white man came to get me. He gave me rough clothing I had never seen before and he put a rope on my hands and bound my hands and feet so that I could not run away, could not hide. I had no strength left to run, no idea where to hide and I knew that I would never see my home again, never see my family, never hunt the animals that were our life and never be warm again.

"There was another man in the cart bound hand and foot like me. He was my sworn enemy. But he was bound too. He was going where I was going. However, I was so tired I didn't care.

"We rode in that cart for I don't know how long. Finally, it was dark, and we came to a very large hut that did not move. I could still see the water off in the distance, but this hut was not in the water. I was given food and even though I did not know what I was eating, I swallowed it. There were many, many other men in this room. We were all locked into the hut. We could not escape this place.

"The next day, I was washed, given more food, and was shown work that I was to do. I also saw a white man who seemed angry and then I saw them, the others, my sworn enemies."

Tribal Enemies

This man's dissertation on his arrival in the

early colonies as a slave continued and he shared information that I had never previously heard anyone ever speak of (and I grew up in the South.) I felt that he had unknowingly waited for someone who could hear his story.

"The evil ones are here! I see them over there. I am sworn to kill them if I see them! This is the way of our tribe, we kill them; they kill us. I have to be careful or they will kill me.

"I see someone from a neighboring tribe; a tribe that we trade with and I ask what is happening. He explains that we are slaves, bought and sold like animals, to work these lands for these white men. He tells me to be careful of the rival tribes. We band together for protection. We know we have to find a way to kill those other men.

"We are proud men. We do not want to wear the clothes the white man tries to force us to wear even though it is cold. Sometimes in the night, men die of the cold. But I am strong. I am stronger than the cold. I do not understand the trees here either. One day the leaves are green, then they are yellow and then they are gone. What kind of an evil trick is this?

"What kind of evil is it that white cold falls out of the sky? I am cold all the time and the food is terrible and I am afraid all the time.

"Many nights, one evil tribe tries to find a way to kill one of us. There is murder very often. Then the white man hangs the tribal man who did the murder. There is much death here.

"Then one day, the white man brings in new people, women. There were women from my old village and women from the village of my enemy. I was afraid for the women of my village. My enemy can never be trusted. Our women are in danger.

"The night the women from our tribe got here, my enemy raped them! We will be sure to rape the women from their village. Vengeance is important to uphold tribal honor. This will put one of our own in their tribe. Then no one will want this woman now because she is defiled: she is ruined."

"Can you tell me if the plantation owners knew anything about these rapes of your women or why there were so many murders on the plantation?"

"No, white man does not understand that we are from all different tribes. Not all tribes can work together. Finally, he figures it out because he begins to separate us by tribe. There are fewer murders and our women are finally safer."

Perhaps the slave traders had unhappy customers, so they began to separate slaves by tribe and men from certain tribes brought more money than others and became highly prized. The slave trade picked up after this.

Collecting Souls

I realized that these ghostly tribes were still ready to murder each other, even in death. So, it immediately became necessary to separate them into tribal groups to even hope to move them to the Heaven World. Once I was able to do this, then the groups over numerous generations began to gather by tribe. I brought in Angels to help them and many hundreds of slaves were guided into the light of the Divine. Men, women, and children who were raped, murdered by a wide variety of ways by both white and black men were released from the unrelenting fear of mortal life and the cold, cruel darkness of tragic death. The dead of many surrounding plantations also seemed to find this welcoming light.

None of them said a word. They all still seemed baffled by what happened to them in life and death. Some were born into slavery in the colonies, on the plantations and knew nothing else. Their only connection to Africa was the stories, the songs and the oral history of their tribe that was passed down or that their families attempted to pass down. The dissolution of thousands of African families created deep emotional scars that have lasted for generations.

Trading Lives of Poverty

They were sometimes called 'indentures' as a shortened form of the term indentured servant. These were the people who, on the social hierarchy, were barely above slave level. These were the English men and women who had nothing else to live for, signed many years of their lives over to a plantation owner in a desperate attempt to escape the grinding poverty of England. This made them virtual slaves to the plantation owner in order to pay for their way to the New World. Each hoped for eventual independence, for a piece of land and the opportunity to enjoy the freedom that being out of England, Ireland, Scotland, and Wales offered.

Her name was Judith Whitcombe, and she seemed more than willing to share her experiences of her life on Berkeley Plantation.

"What do you do when you have nothing left to live for, no hope that tomorrow will ever change? Filth, that is the only way to describe debtor's prison. Everything was dirty all the time, and cruel.

"We knew families who had gone to debtor's prison. They never came out. We saw them, their thin, filthy arms outstretched through the prison iron bars, begging for relief. I was terrified that this would happen to us. We had nothing. Our fledgling leather business failed. We had no money for food. No one would hire my husband, William. We were starving to death. These were desperate times.

"The day we went to court, someone came in who was a representative for the colonies. He said he would take anyone about to be sentenced to debtor's prison to the New World as an indentured servant. He said he would even take couples.

"William and I had heard that this could happen, and we decided that, given the opportunity, we would take it. We figured that a couple without children might be picked over another family with little ones. That's harsh, I know. I feel bad saying that but . . . these were such anxious times. But hope, even that slim glimpse of hope, if that's all you have, makes people do desperate things.

"The Crown judge sentenced us to indentured servitude to a plantation owner in the Virginia colony for seven years. But we weren't the only ones that day. Several families went too, even ones with babies and children. I figured they wanted all kinds of helping hands in this new world. At least William's ability to make things out of leather could readily be used and I can sew, so I could sew the things he could make."

Eating and Sleeping with Fear

"I'm so sorry things were so difficult for you, Judith. How did you fair on the crossing? Were you and your companions alright?"

"Most of the indentures on our ship died on the passage over. We were sickly to begin with, not much food to eat before we left. Most of us were skin and bones when we started out. We retched for days. Some simply fell overboard in the heavy seas as they were retching. Maybe they wished they could die. We all felt that bad. There weren't enough provisions on the ship and it often washed overboard in the storms that seemed to plague us.

"It was heartbreaking: the babies died first, then the little children then the women and some of the men. I don't know how or why I survived. Maybe it would have been better if I had died at sea . . .

"William and I believed that once we arrived in Virginia, somehow things would be so much better. But we had no idea how hard it would be for us. I cannot begin to tell you how crushing the reality of disappointment became. We had gone from one grim situation to another. The few of us who survived the trip and then went to a plantation found ourselves treated no better than the Negro slaves who worked side by side with us. The only advantage we had was that we spoke the same language as the plantation owners. But even that mattered little: we were all at the mercy of our 'owners' for all of our needs. We were given the bare minimum of food to survive day-to-day. That bare minimum was just not enough for some of us. Disease was rampant. There was no medical care and there was little food. If the plantation couldn't grow it, raise it as chickens, a cow or two, or hunt it, we couldn't eat it. Sometimes we were given our own plots to try to grow food, but we were often too exhausted to tend them.

"Some indentures were so poorly treated that they ran away in desperation. We all wanted to run away, but life outside of the plantation wasn't going to be any easier. The indentures that did escape were considered thieves because they owed years to the plantation owners, which they had no hope of ever repaying. Some of them were hung as thieves. It was demoralizing."

"Did you ever have children? Did you and William want children?"

"Oh yes, I would have loved a child, but there wasn't enough food for me and a baby. I prayed that I would never get pregnant. The work was so grueling. We women indentures helped with everything that our masters demanded, including working on construction projects. We suffered the cold, the harsh winters and the dripping, humid summers with the insects that you couldn't see that ate you alive. But the worst was the cruel gnawing of being constantly hungry. Sometimes I wondered what it would be like not to be starving.

"So many things were new for us, foreign, and utterly frightening. We were absolutely terrified of the Indians. The stories of what could happen to white indentured servants at the hands of the Indians, was so terrorizing, that some of us believed we would surely die of fright."

"Were there Indian attacks or were the plantations secure enough that you could be safe working there?"

"Oh my God, yes, the Indians attacked! Sometimes they would come whooping at us with these ghastly painted faces and snatch a woman in the fields. Sometimes, we would never see her again. I was terrified every day. When one woman didn't come back one night, we knew something horrible had happened to her, but we didn't know if it was wolves or Indians. The next morning, we found her hacked-up body in the field. She had such beautiful blonde hair and it was gone. She was attacked and scalped in the field; I had never seen a person's body that had been scalped. It isn't an image I can get to leave my head. It was horrible."

Judith begins to cry, those deep almost paralyzing sobs that come from unspent grief, exhaustion, and the destruction of hope. But once she started, she wanted to tell me her whole story, or as much as she could get out. Her waif thin body and her shredded clothes suggested that something very brutal happened to her. She continued.

"We had never seen people with skin that color, that black, black color. We were so frightened of them. I was terrified to even touch them. Some of the men had a wild look in their eyes and they spoke a language I had never heard. We could not communicate with them. They were fighting each other sometimes. We did not understand them, yet we were expected to work side-by-side with them. I was afraid day and night. William was so exhausted that I had no hope that he would be able to protect me from all of these terrifying things. How can anyone live in this new world, this new hell?

"We were glad when the plantation owner brought over new women, so that we could befriend them, but at the same time, we knew their lives wouldn't be any better here. But we welcomed each new woman who arrived with warmth and compassion because it is always easier to face extreme duress when you don't have to do it alone. And eventually there were enough of us that we didn't feel quite so lonely anymore in our misery. At least we could be in it together. Sometimes we hugged each other

140

in the fields just to be warm.

"Plantation owners were harsh. There was never a kind word to us. We worked seven days a week. Our clothes had to be completely shredded before we were allowed to make something new for ourselves. Wool was scarce. We couldn't knit something without wool, and we had no money to buy wool from a trader. Food was carefully managed. There was never enough to eat.

"The weather was hot and sticky, or brutally cold, so cold, I often wished that I could slip inside a snowbank and just go to sleep and wake up in Heaven. This is a cruel place. The plantation owners are cruel, the Indians kill us, the dark people terrify us, and the weather brutalizes us. Wouldn't death be better?"

Death visited Berkeley Plantation often.

"If someone had told you and William what conditions were like here, Judith, would you both still have come?"

"We asked ourselves this again and again. Once people arrived here, no one ever returned to England. No one ever told us what it was like to be an indentured servant. We realized that when you are poor, that there are no options. William and I sometimes prayed for death so that we could escape this hell, but we didn't want to abandon each other. I guess

I would have to say that the only warmth we ever truly felt was when we were in bed hugging each other.

"I would have died much sooner had William not been by my side. I couldn't imagine what it would have been like to live there with children. Each baby, each child that died broke my heart. Their mothers had no time to grieve them. After your child died, burial was immediate and then you went right back to work, crying through your chores, sobbing yourself to sleep and losing the desire to eat. Death visited Berkeley Plantation often."

Judith spoke this last sentence flatly, as if that reality was almost a shadow self, an ever-present eventuality.

"Forgive me for asking this, but do you know that death did finally come for you and William?"

"Yes, we know we're dead. All of us, we know it. I can see the other women, the men, even some of the Negroes, and even some of the dead plantation owners. How can it be that even in death we are still together?"

"Did you have any type of belief system?"

"Yes, we did. We all prayed every day, but I guess it didn't matter. We figured God abandoned this new world.

"Winter was especially horrible one year: it seemed to last forever, and provisions were lean. We had hunted the surrounding area to the point that I guess the men had to keep going out farther and farther and were gone longer and longer. On one of those trips, William just didn't come back. The other men said that he fell from his horse and died on the march. They buried him somewhere in the woods because they had to bring the food back on the horses. They had no space to carry a body. There was no Christian burial for my sweet husband. I guess my heart broke after that. William kept me alive. Without his love, his kind face there was nothing left to live for. That year the plantation grieved the loss of five children to the cold and sickness. I couldn't take any more grief."

". . . being with him dead . . ."

"I only wanted to be with William. After William died, I - I guess I wasn't much good for anything, so they made me go out into the woods and pick up kindling for the kitchen house, kettle fire. It was a dusky November night. I got lost or, or maybe I just couldn't go back. I don't know. I remember tripping over something in the darkness and I remember falling and then blackness, dense blackness. Finally, I found William, so I figured out I died. I'm still cold but being with him dead is better than being without him alive. Then I began to see other indentures. I guess that's the end of my story. It's not a very good story but it's what happened to me, to us. It feels like I died yesterday. Can you help us? Will you help us?"

Her voice, barely above a whisper seemed to trail off as she ended her tale of life on Berkeley Plantation. Grief permeated her soul. Involuntarily I took a deep breath.

"Yes, absolutely, Judith. See here, I've brought in all of these beautiful angels to help you. I've asked each angel to give you all nourishing food and to wrap you in the warmth of these soft, comforting blankets. Are you beginning to feel this warmth?"

There were thousands of these indentured servants waiting for help. All of them were freezing, and bone weary from the life just lived. The warmth of the Divine light was the first comfortable moment many had experienced since leaving England many centuries ago. The angels transitioned all who were present from that harsh yet critical period of American history.

Shirley Plantation

All the souls who asked for help once I left Berkeley Plantation were transitioned. Nearby Shirley Plantation was my next stop on this meaningful stroll through history. Shirley is the oldest plantation in Virginia, founded in 1613, only six years after the first permanent English settlement at Jamestown. This plantation was and still is owned by descendants of the Hill family, many of whom, currently reside in the magnificent mansion built in 1723.

Visitors are invited to tour the lush grounds as well as the main home. I did not enter the main house as the afternoon was waning. As my steps traced those of the owners on the handmade brick paths that wind their way through modest English-style formal gardens, I slipped into a dreamy moment. Fragrant rose bushes, old-fashioned box woods and giant pin oaks lined the walkways. It is easy to lose yourself here, to imagine walking in the shoes of some past inhabitant of this lovely farm, who might have also walked through here, heading to the bountiful garden. Turning around I began gazing at the main plantation house pondering whether or not the thick-looking glass was original in those windows, and that's when I saw her.

There was a fierce looking grandmother figure staring back at me from an upstairs bedroom window. Instantly, my wistful moment was gone. I drew back, immediately feeling like an unwanted intruder into a world that was not my own but was definitely hers.

I caught her watching with a most stern look on her face. She wore a loose white, elegantly embroidered nightgown and a nightcap with the under-chin ties undone. I doubt that anyone else saw her aged face. Her ghostly visage was only there briefly and then she was gone. But I could hear her telling me that theirs was a better-run plantation than Berkeley. She must have been listening to the other transitioning souls.

"Who are you?"

"We own this plantation! We make everyone work extremely hard so that the plantation makes money and so that we are always self-sufficient. We grow our own cotton and flax to make our clothing, all of our own food. We have smoke houses to store meat when game is lean.

"Those indentures and those slaves will tell you that we were harsh, that we were cruel here, but we had to be strict in order to survive the winters. Some of the indentures were lazy. The Negroes didn't know what to do and they only understood our authority if we were tough."

"Did things ever get better? The reality was that you all had to work together to survive. Was it necessary to be that cruel, to deprive these people of all hope?"

"These are the proper ways to manage the staff."

Yes, it was what was done. It was the culture of that time. But the slaves were on that plantation for generations. Some of these

146

ancestors of the original slaves still walk these paths, the ones they walked in life and in death. Even the slaves here on Shirley Plantation feel that the mortal visitors do not belong. Maybe the dead feel that this is hallowed ground. It is hard to say.

"Would you tell me your name? What happened to you?"

"My name is none of your business, and nothing happened to me. I am still managing this plantation. You are an intruder."

As she spoke to me, I guessed that she simply went to sleep and never realized that she died. Her fierce independence, arrogance and power suggested she would go on for eternity managing that plantation.

I can feel that there are more dead here, souls who have walked this land for over 400 years. I think some of them are family members, like the grandmother who was steadily watching from the upstairs bedroom. I have this uneasy feeling that none of them like visitors and none are necessarily ready to transition to the Heaven World.

Epilogue

Both Berkeley and Shirley Plantations are privately owned. Therefore, when I am at a private location and begin to leave and notice that the dead still follow me, I have to wait until I am on public property to help them. I can then move on those dead souls, for permission from a particular property owner is not required.

The cruel irony of this concept was not lost on me: I would still have to have the permission of the property owners to help both the slave and indentured souls. I felt myself shudder inwardly. The traces of slavery transcended time and space in this situation. But, once on public property, I can freely help any soul who follows me and asks for help. As soon as I set foot on the road in front of the house, I was then free to cross over all souls who requested the assistance or who had followed me. It felt good to be able to address this spiritually critical need.

All of the souls: Native Americans, plantation owners, slaves, and indentures from both plantations, who asked for help, were afforded the light of the Divine. As I write this statement, it seems flat, unemotional and without depth, yet several thousand souls from these two plantations, over several hundred years crossed over.

People forget that there were children born to both slaves and indentured servants , eventually. They all need the consoling energy of the divine.

Crossing over is never anti-climactic for the soul. It is always joyous. These souls have been denied the comfort of the Divine for over 400 years. While it is wonderful to be able to help them, it is also disheartening to think how long a wait that is for the soul who is chilled and fearful, lonely, and confused. Yes, time does not exist for them; there are no visible 'time you have been dead clocks' to advise a soul how long he or she has wandered in this gloom. Yet, there is a subtle feeling, an aching longing to be free to find the light.

The Smell of Revenge

A friend of mine from Georgia called and chatted for a few minutes and then blurted out this – shall we say – somewhat odd question.

"Do you do smells? I mean can you do whatever it is that you do and get rid of a smell in someone's home? Is it possible to have a psychic smell?"

"Yes, there is such a thing as a psychic smell and, frankly, it is among the hardest to remove because there is a vagueness to the entire situation. That vagueness makes it very challenging for any psychic to find it, much less remove it, so I can definitely look at your place, but I can't offer any guarantees. Nothing in the etheric world of the 4th dimension can ever be guaranteed."

"Well, I need you to do somethin' because this smell is drivin' me nuts. I just moved into this apartment. I love it here; it's close to work, has nice people and seems to be great, except for this horrible smell! It comes from everywhere and nowhere. I've checked plumbin', garbage, and toilets. I even had a plumber come out to check for weird gases. Then I had the gas company come out and they couldn't find a thing. It smells bad but it isn't gas. I don't even know how to describe it. It's just awful.

"Oh, and this smell comes and goes. There is absolutely no rhyme or reason to it. And it nags at me, like I have to do something about this. I don't know what to call it, this energy that I can smell, but not see.

"Look, I know in the world of whatever it is that you actually do, that there are no guarantees, but I really need help with this. Here's my new address."

When the Dogs Talk, You Listen

I readily located my friend's apartment and found absolutely nothing. No ghost or a dark intelligence could be found. I could not actually smell anything in the ether, the world of the 4th dimension. This is precisely why psychic smells are so frustrating to resolve and remove.

Then I remembered that she had dogs and dogs know all about smell, so I did something

I had never done before: I asked her dogs where the smell was originating. Her dogs were amazing. They knew exactly where the smell came from and told me that it was from the apartment below them. They were more than happy to help because, ever the loyal creatures, they wanted to help their owner and the smell was bothering them, too. No creature likes an irritable owner!

Death without Dignity

I was greatly relieved to know where the smell originated but then that created another problem. I had no spiritual jurisdiction to clear the apartment below my client's. You cannot just knock on someone's door and ask if you can psychically look at his or her home. So, I decided to offset the smell by doing something to attract whatever was creating it and haunting the apartment below my client. Ghosts are not encumbered by location, so I decided to try to lure the ghost to me.

Souls often miss the material gratifications of being in a physical world, so, in the 4th dimension, I created a healing circle with soft blankets, some deliciously warm and aromatic bread with fresh butter and jam. When you create something that satisfies the longing of the dead to have that sensation of savoring the fleeting pleasures of being in a physical body, you can get their attention.

Then I sent out a psychic message that anyone who had need of healing or food could come and visit my healing circle. I had no idea who or what would arrive, just that this has worked in the past and was worth trying again.

"I did not die a good death."

Sure enough, a young woman in her twenties arrived. She was wearing clothing indicating she died in the late 20th or early 21st century. She stepped right into that circle and went after the blanket and the bread. While she was happily munching, I asked her if she was aware that she was dead.

"Of course, I know I'm dead! Don't you think I would much rather be out shopping, or working at my job than talking to you from wherever in whatever world I'm actually in? Maybe if I could have lived a long life and died a good death, I might know what to do now but I don't because I didn't die a good death!"

When she said this last sentence, it was as if she emphasized each word. This concept of dying a good death was so important to her that she wanted to be sure that I 'got it,' that her death was not good.

"Why would you think you didn't die a good death? What happened that caused your death? You must have been such a pretty young woman." And she might have been lovely, except in the ashen condition she presented to me, she seemed thin, haggard and the look on her face seemed as if she was still in some level of pain. She was wearing an ugly, open-backed hospital gown.

"Death with dignity is something every person should experience. But there was no dignity in my death. It was horrible. You know? I believe that I was murdered, but not the way that you could get the police to investigate. I just know he killed me. He did it!"

"I'm sorry, what's your name?"

"Gay Lynn, everyone called me Gayly, with the Ly as part of Lynn. I know it's an odd name, but I loved it. I was a happy person! Happy until he came along and KILLED ME!"

"I'm so sorry this happened to you. How horrifying! Please tell me what actually occurred? How did he do it?"

"I rotted from the inside out. The doctors were baffled by this bizarre infection. I just know Mac did this to me, caused me to die this way. I mean, you know, I was fine, healthy as a horse, busy, athletic, doing all kinds of things and then, you know, I realized that Mac wasn't the guy for me. I tried to make our breakup amicable, you know they use that word for breakups that are supposed to be friendly, but it wasn't that friendly.

"He begged me to stay and try to make it

work. So, I did, but I was watching the days go by and, you know, I guess I fell out of love with him. It happens. There wasn't anybody else but something about Mac started to feel off. You know what I mean? Off, like he wasn't the guy for me, and I talked to my girlfriends, and they all said just dump him, you know? Dump him and move on; you're young and cute and there are lots of guys out there and we talked about it over and over. And then it started."

"What started? What happened?"

"Well, as I started packing my things, to move out, he asked me to stay one more week, sort of like, to try one more time. So, I did and right away, I started to feel bad when this headache started and OMG, my stomach hurt so much! You know you get used to feeling great and this hit me out of nowhere. As the days went on, I got some type of infection. But how? I never left the house. The doctors said that I had a 'massive putrid infection.' Basically, all my organs were beginning to rot from the inside out."

"Wow, that's incredible. Did they have a name for this kind of infection or how you contracted such a terrible illness?"

"No, that's just the thing – no one could figure it out. They knew my organs were full of this bizarre infection, but no antibiotic would touch it. You ever hear of flesh-eating bacteria? Well, this was working on the inside of my body, which is why they said it was so weird. I hadn't left the country, met any mysterious strangers, nothin', and yet all of a sudden, I get this bizarre infection. BIZARRE! The doctors used that word over and over as if – I don't know – somebody used black magic on me, or somethin'. I was pissed. I had a life, you know? I didn't initially hate Mac but after a while, when your stomach is rotting from the inside out you get the feeling that he knows something he isn't telling anybody and then all of a sudden, I died! I overheard the doctors say it was septisomethin' and that I had – let's see . . . what did he call it? Oh, catastrophic failure of all of my organs and even as this baffled doctor is standing over my dead body in that hospital room, he still can't figure out what killed me. You know, you'd think that a doctor would know more than this, Lord knows they did every test in the book on me and I STILL DIED!"

"No wonder you're so upset! What happened after you died? Did you get any idea of how Mac supposedly killed you, what he used, how he did it?"

"No, that's the weird part. He acted all broken up, like, you know, he cared about me. He didn't give anybody a clue. I listened. I went to my funeral and he never said a bad thing about me. But there was this part of me that, you know, I just knew he did it. He put

157

somethin' horrible in my food or somethin' and he killed me."

Revenge from the Grave

"I'm just curious, once you went to your funeral, did you see a light? Could you have crossed over into that light?"

"Yeah, I guess I could have, but I was way too intent on getting my revenge on him. I decided that since he wanted me so bad in life that by God, he was going to have me forever haunting him in death. I was going to have my vengeance. Oh, that light, maybe I saw it, maybe not. I wasn't interested in going anywhere. I just wanted to haunt him, to make him pay."

"How did you get your revenge on him? What did you do to him?"

"I decided to create this awful putrid smell, the smell of my death. This is my plan of harassing him from the grave. I also watch him as he goes about his days. He isn't with anyone else yet, because maybe he can't get rid of this smell. I created the smell my body gave off as I was dying, the smell of my death – that I just know he caused."

"Did you realize that as you stick with him in death to get revenge that he is also keeping you a prisoner in death as well. Did you ever look at it this way?"

"No, I never looked at it that way. I don't want to be his prisoner anymore, you know, but I'm so angry!"

"Do you realize that other people in other apartments near this one, can smell that horrible smell too, and that you are unintentionally punishing them as well?"

"No. I had no idea. Is that why you're here? Does it have to do with the smell?"

"Yes, it does. The owner of the apartment above your boyfriend's has tried everything to get rid of this smell. She asked me to help her with it and that's how I found you. Can your boyfriend smell it, too? Are you getting the revenge you wanted, GayLy? How is this working for you, this smell of revenge thing you've got going on?"

"I can't tell if it's botherin' him at all you know? He doesn't even seem to notice it and it takes a lot of my energy to do this. But nothing works. He just goes about his life. His life. He still has a life, I don't. I have nothin' but my revenge."

"So, are you tired yet? Are you ready for this to be over? Would you accept some help finding the light and being released from Mac? Are you ready to finally break free of him?"

"Yeah, I guess I'm ready. I feel so empty inside; like that putrid infection destroyed what was good in me. Am I a bad person? Do you think Jesus will let me come home?"

"Absolutely, which is precisely why I have brought this sweet angel to guide you across that light bridge. I have it on good authority that someone will meet you and welcome you home. It's time."

The angel took her hand and they crossed over. She was smiling as she left.

Epilogue

I went back and 'talked' with the dogs to verify that the smell had in fact left. They informed me that the smell was gone and then later when I spoke with my friend, she also confirmed that the smell "is completely gone – finally!"

Whether or not Mac caused her infection, GayLy believed he did. The irony was that it was that putrid smell that eventually enabled her to be released.

The Orphanage

Being psychic has always had its challenges, but never more so than for an intuitive young woman named Victoria. This young woman learned early on how to deal with the unusual number of ghosts who seem to be attracted to her. She learned how to protect herself from ghosts, and how to assist them to cross over to the Heaven World. One of Victoria's experiences, which occurred when she was a freshman in college, stands out.

"It was around 2:45pm on Tuesday, Dec. 4, 2012. I was sitting in my History of England class when I started to get a pain in my stomach. I thought it was just a random pain. A few minutes later I started to feel very weird, lightheaded, and my vision blurred. I felt an urgency to get out of the classroom. As I walked down the hall to get to the bathroom, I started to black out. My ears muted and I was shivery. I thought I was turning into the bathroom, but I became disoriented and somehow ended up running into the wall next to the bathroom door and bloodied my nose. It strongly felt as if someone had pushed me into the wall, but there was no one there.

"I was eventually able to make it into the bathroom and I started putting cold water on my face, neck, and wrists. I felt faint for several minutes. I started to use all the tools I could think of to protect myself from anything that I suspected was with me. I realized something about this situation was different from any other psychic situation I had been in before. Having learned how to help ghosts find the light, I say The Crossing Over Prayer whenever I feel the need. I tried it here, but something about this situation was different.

"I felt that I had been attacked and I asked for angels of protection and transition, but it still took a couple of minutes to feel good enough to return to class. I realized that I had been out of class, struggling with this for about 30 minutes total. During the rest of the class period, I found myself unable to concentrate on the lecture. When class was over, I called Tina to see if she could help me figure out what had happened.

"Tina and I worked together in a meditation and found out that I did have 'someone' with me. A ghostly young woman named Mary had tried very hard to get my attention. Tina said that Mary had used all of her other dimensional energy to break through my layers of protection in order to get my attention so that I could help her. This was why I was so dizzy and disoriented that I ran into the wall, which was how I ended up with a bloody nose. After talking to Tina, we found out that Mary had an incredible story to tell. This is what she shared with me."

Through Multiple Dimensions and Stacks of Time: Victoria Shares Mary's Story

"Mary was a young woman who died in a car crash some years ago. She was a history major with a special interest in colonial times. It just so happened that we were discussing the colonial period in my History of England class.

"After Mary died in that car crash around the year 2001, she told us that she could immediately see a few ghostly souls who died in the 1600s. Tina told me that this was quite unusual: souls from modern times usually cannot see souls from past times. Mary would have had to have a special affinity to that time to be able to see them, and as it turns out, she did. She recognized a group of souls from that time period who she knew personally. I couldn't understand how that could happen. Tina explained that this was some weird type of group karma, meaning I guess, that Mary had a special connection to these ghosts. I sensed this was going to get even more interesting because Mary was desperate to get help not only for herself, but she also wanted help for those souls too."

The Greatest Act of Kindness

"Now the story gets even weirder. We discovered that Mary had had a life during the exact period that these 'colonial' ghosts had lived. She knew these people; she had grown up with them. Mary was especially close to a woman, now a ghost, by the name of Abigail Seward who had acted as a mother to her. Now, I will try to explain the complicated story that I learned. I know it's a little convoluted, but this is Mary's story as she explained it to me.

"They were Quakers but to be socially accepted, they converted to the Puritan belief. This couple fully integrated into the settlement and they were considered very hard workers. The people in this settlement knew they had to stick together because times were so tough. Food was chronically scarce and merely surviving day-to-day was their constant challenge.

"One day, Abigail's husband went out on an exploration mission with several other men and the entire group of men never returned home. Her husband went missing or died just after she had given birth to their third child. All of a sudden Abigail had no one to support her. It was then that she looked around and noticed that there were more children than she had realized who needed the same type of help that she did: someone to support them. Other families were taking these children in, but they were becoming taxed and tired. Abigail decided to start an orphanage for the children whose parents had died either during the voyage from England, from death while hunting, or from sickness or childbirth in the new world. She was able to run the home because the entire village helped her out by sharing food, clothing, and firewood.

"As it turns out, Mary, our modern-day ghost, had reincarnated from this period. During the life she had in the 1600s, she was one of those children who lost both of her parents and had no place to live. Abigail adopted her and became her 'mother' when Mary was in her early teens.

"Abigail always seemed to be there for Mary, including helping Mary find a husband in a neighboring village. These two women were extremely close. Eventually, Mary and her husband moved to another village to start their life. Meanwhile, Abigail continued to embrace all the orphaned children in the village."

The Cruelest Act of Greed: An Officer of the Crown

"Mary continued to share with me how this fledgling settlement started with glorious hopes and dreams. She said that they were such good people and they all worked side-by-side to make the settlement work. However, what she told me next changed their lives forever.

"England always seemed to have an officer of the Crown in one village or another to make sure that any goods or money due to the Crown were collected and returned to England. Samuel Stevens, an officer in the King's army until around 1640, was the collector of all that was due to the Crown.

"Samuel was blindly loyal to the Crown. At some point, he became increasingly irritated that the villagers were spending their time and money to provide for the orphan children instead of providing things to make money for King Charles I and England. Tina and I were never able to understand why he was so bothered by the fact that the villagers supported the orphanage, but he was. Apparently, his irritation turned to anger, and his anger turned to rage. We may never know what pressure he was under to send money to the Crown. We will never understand what possessed him, for surely, he could not have thought of this on his own. Maybe we don't want to know. Samuel Stevens was one of history's unknown agents of unspeakable viciousness.

"We do not know if this happened during the evening or the dead of night. Nor do we know what was going through his mind at the time. We don't know if he thought about the results of his actions.

"What we do know is that Samuel Stevens burned down Abigail's orphanage, killing Abigail and most of the roughly 30 children in her care who were in that house at that moment. We believe that some children were with other families that night because not all the children died.

"This early, primitive settlement had no way to fight such a fire. They all stood there horrified, with no way to rescue the people who were dying in that little structure. The children had no way to get out. I would imagine that the bloodcurdling screams of those dying children lived in the hearts and minds of that settlement for a very long time. The gruesome nature of this act sickened and depressed the entire settlement. The grief they all felt lingered in the air like a thick black, blanketing fog that enveloped them, haunting their days and nights without end. The children weren't merely orphans; they were the sons and daughters of the settlement, their hope for tomorrow.

"We don't know if the settlement knew that Samuel committed this mass murder. At first, we suspected that Samuel felt terrible about his actions, but he felt he could still justify his heinous act by the fact that he was trying to make more money for his country. A few weeks later, a supply ship came bearing the news that the monarchy had been abolished and the King had been killed during the English Civil War (1649/50). To his horror, Samuel then realized that what he had done had no point or meaning, since the motive behind his actions, to make money for King and country, no longer existed.

"Here is a man who seemingly had no conscience, yet he committed suicide with a shot to the brain. Maybe he felt he could no longer live with his murderous deeds; maybe he felt he should be punished.

"I asked Tina about moving on Samuel Stevens to the appropriate realm in the Heaven World. I guess some people would think that it would have made sense to leave him in the hell of his own making. But she said that the negativity that that particular stack of time was emitting had to be cleaned up, and that included all souls involved with the tragic situation. So, she moved him on to what she called the 'appropriate realm' in the Heaven World. Tina said this is a place where very evil people go to balance the karma they created in this life. I had often wondered what happens on the other side to people like him."

Healing Across the Stacks of Time

"Tina and I turned our attention to Abigail and all those dead children. We realized that when Abigail died, she was confused and did not know if they should move on in the Quaker or Puritan belief. Her confusion literally left her stuck in that terrible darkness for over 400 years. Perhaps neither faith would have helped her understand what to do after death because as Tina explained, there is no religion in the afterlife.

"Mary, our modern-day ghost, and guide in this bizarre 1600s scenario, told us that after the horrific method that caused Abigail's death, she returned with her husband from that other village to help out the town. She grieved her adopted 'mother' tremendously and vowed to help the remaining children who had not died in the ghastly fire. After many years of dedicated service of running the orphanage, Mary died, and she must have moved immediately into the light. She would not have seen Abigail and the children at that time because none of them had moved into the light after the fire. This was the entire reason for Mary to ask for help: those souls from that fire were still there, waiting for help to find the light, for the energy of the fire kept them in that terrible place all that time.

"I thought this was an amazing validation of the concepts that Tina has taught me about resonance. The final irony is that Mary died near the place where her adoptive family had been murdered 400 years prior and sought to help them all. That place was at a small college in Virginia. Through an odd quirk of fate, she was able to somehow reach back through time and find 'her family' when she died. She had such love and dedication to her adoptive family that she could sense that they needed help so many years later."

Epilogue

Victoria's story reminds us that love never dies, and that deep affection transcends time. It is indeed perplexing to understand the mind-warping concept of a ghost who died in the 21st century reaching back to help ghosts of roughly 400 years ago. Perhaps Mary realized upon her own death that those souls from that stack of time were stuck and vowed she would help them somehow. It's also possible she was able to actually see these 17th century ghosts as she was living her 21st century life.

Ghosts do not always share the background information provided in these situations. Angels sent to assist from the Heaven World afford much of the background information provided to me.

This story goes to show that, no matter how much you may think you know about helping the dead, sometimes, things happen in such a way that you end up learning how to help those unhappy souls on a whole new level.

Anything is possible in the world of the dead. Our college student will never look at the world of living and dying the same again. If nothing else, she will more fully embrace the concept that biology does not make a family, and that love transcends time and space.

The Yorktown Cemetery

You expect ghosts at a century old war cemetery in Virginia.

You expect the headstones to tell the name and date of the warrior's death.

You expect to see visitors at any historical cemetery, noting the passage of so many lives. You could reasonably anticipate the stereotypical types of visitors: you know, the curious, the historians, long lost relatives.

Well, so much for expectations . . .

Remembrance

It's hard to believe that a place as beautiful as Yorktown could be the site of so much bloody history. The charming homes in this tiny town next to Colonial National Historical Park bear no evidence that so many key battles of the Revolutionary War were fought there. Civil War battles were fought in

Yorktown and Williamsburg, too. In fact, Yorktown has a very modest sized Civil War Cemetery, and while visiting this lovely area with my family, we stumbled upon this graveyard.

There is a commemorative plaque at the entrance to this neatly kept cemetery, that invites you to pay homage to the Civil War dead of both sides who are buried here. I even found one of my own relatives resting there. That alone felt strange, poignant almost, offering me an unnerving connection to the past. This particular cemetery is the final resting place for roughly 1600 Civil War soldiers. Of this number only 747 of them have their names listed on that commemorative plaque. The others, the men who will forever remain unknown, are remembered only by the few 'remains' that were left to bury.

'Remains.' This cold, flat, unemotional word is the term we use for the leftovers of the unidentified souls lost in war, shattered by cannon blasts and land mines. Land mines were the cruel surprises the Confederacy left behind for unsuspecting Union soldiers marching through Yorktown. There was never much left of these men except body parts or pieces clad in shredded blue uniforms.

The Sentinel Cedar Tree

There was a tremendous cedar tree growing nearby, standing at attention: watching over the dead. Cedar trees grow slowly. So slowly, that a two-hundred-year-old cedar would not look much larger than a fifty-year-old oak tree. It is hard to gauge just how old any cedar is. Some can grow to be over 800 years old. The stoic looking sentinel cedar tree in the Yorktown Civil War Cemetery seemed to be roughly two hundred and fifty years old, perhaps older. Its mildly shredded, ruddy-colored bark was a perfect foil for the deep green of its short, bundled needles. Trees anchor time, and this cedar tree seemed to be a likely anchor for both the Revolutionary and Civil War. Several other tall guardian trees were sparsely spread out among the headstones of this national cemetery and burial ground so near Revolutionary War battle sites. There were quite a few Civil War battles fought near Yorktown, including the Battles of Yorktown and Williamsburg where 3900 Confederate and Union soldiers lost their lives.

I placed my hand on the soft bark of this enduring tree and pondered the story it had to tell. This guardian projected a patient presence, almost a kind personality that seemed to be 'watching over the dead' buried there.

The Visitors: Abigail, Charlotte, Ashley. .
.

"Why, Fredrick? Why didn't you come back to me? You promised me you'd come back and marry me. I was supposed to be Mrs. Abigail Johnson. I scoured the lists of dead every day. I never saw your name. I hoped and I prayed for you, I asked Jesus to protect you. Did you hear my prayers for you? Did you know how much I loved you? Did you have to fight in this stupid war? When they said the war was over, I kept expecting to see you. Finally, your name was on the very last list. How could you do this to me? How could you survive the whole war and then end up dead? Why? How did this happen? Oh my God, I miss you so much!"

The tree seemed to narrate. Perhaps narrate is the wrong word. Touching the tree caused me to be gently guided back through time, back through the more recent ages offering me a glimpse of an historic reality and enabling me to see and hear them – the visitors. These visitors to this graveyard came to grieve in the days after 1865, after the Civil War was over.

They were so uniquely dressed, each of them, from their particular social class. I did not want to disturb them as I watched, yet I could distinctly hear what they were each saying.

Abigail was exquisitely attired in a neatly appointed lace draped, cream-colored skirt and blouse. Her puffed sleeves revealing a simple extended sleeve that met her white gloved hand. She was holding a delicate lace handkerchief that was wet with her bitter tears. I would have imagined she would wear black, but she was wearing cream. She was actually lying on the ground in front of the headstone of one of the soldiers, speaking out loud to him as if she desperately hoped that he would answer her back.

"Oh, Fredrick!" She wailed as she gulped in air between her sobs, "How could you leave me? I – I love you so much sometimes I can't breathe. When I try to sleep, I can feel you. I can feel the cold air on your jacket and the smell of your pipe. I can still feel your strong arms holding me close – so close . . ."

Her hair had come undone from its stunning, carved ivory combs and pins. The escaped locks that hid her face were a gorgeous auburn and were damp with her tears.

And she wasn't alone.

Another woman walked up to me and asked if she could show me her brother's grave.

"I'm Helen. My brother died fighting for the Confederacy and when he didn't come home,

Ghost Stories from the Ghosts' Point of View

I came here looking for him. We were so close, only 18 months apart. All we had together was our childhood. It hurts every time I think of all of those wonderful times we shared, his devilish laugh and his curly blonde hair. I think he died at the Battle of Williamsburg. What a waste. He was barely seventeen. I miss him every day."

One by one, the women came forward to tell their stories.

"I'm Joanna. My Dad, my brother and fiancé all died at the Battle of Williamsburg. I got a letter from my fiancé that he somehow mailed from here, so I knew where to look. There's something so final about seeing a fresh grave and a new headstone."

She looked away as tears ran down her face in new rivulets of heartbreak.

"You have to help me: I don't know how to grieve three people. I take turns going to each grave and crying, of talking to them, of letting them know I'm here, but it isn't helping."

"My name's Ashley Cooper. I came up from Savannah to find my husband's grave. I'm stayin' here for a while. There was nothin' much left of Savannah once that devil, General Sherman marched through to the sea. He burned everything in his path. I don't know how the south will ever recover. We lost everything. Why go back? I learned that Billy was in the Battle of Williamsburg – it was the last letter that I got from him so I figured I would try here. I have to find him – find his grave."

Several graves over, I met Charlotte. She wore a plain muslin 'homespun' dress, clean but devoid of any decoration. Her resources appeared to be much less than Abigail's. She also seemed to be older, perhaps thirty or thirty-five.

"Ah, little Lenny, Momma's here. Momma's here my sweet baby, I've come to find you. See, I found you at last. I prayed for you every night to come home."

"Excuse me, ma'am. I couldn't help but hear your conversation. How old was your son? What happened to him?"

"My sweet Lenny was only fourteen when he ran away to be a drummer for the Union Army. He told me how much he wanted to go. I was so worried about his daddy being gone for 4 years already and no word that I begged Lenny not to go. I told him it would break my heart. I told him he was too young to fight, that there were others who could go. I can't run the farm without you I told him. I cried. I remember the determined look on his face.

"I remember that night, when I tried to sleep, I prayed to Jesus not to take my boy, not to leave me so utterly alone and vulnerable.

"The next morning, he was gone. I nearly went mad with worry. At least I found your grave, sweet Lenny, but I can't seem to find you."

"Can you tell me your name?"

"I'm Charlotte Jefferson. We have a farm . . . well, we - we had a farm until I no longer had my husband and son to help me run it. It's tough to manage a hog farm by yourself. I pretty much lost everything. With my husband and boy gone, I felt so broken inside that I couldn't run the farm. I sold what I could to the Union Army, and then I barely survived the war. When the war ended, I watched out every day, hoping, praying my menfolk would come home. After six months, I had to face the hard truth that they weren't ever comin' back.

"I guess I pretty much figured my husband died, but sweet Lenny, without even the hope of ever seeing my sweet Lenny again, I think part of me died inside. I remember one rainy night lying in bed, feeling my heartbeat. I realized that it was just a dull hollow sound that kept me breathing but didn't allow me to feel alive anymore.

"I begged the War Department to help me find out what happened to him. Finally, I got a letter from them in 1867 telling me that he was here, buried in this cemetery.

"At least he got a Christian burial and a proper headstone. I found out my husband Charles died at Antietam at the start of the war. Now, I lost Lenny too. How many tears can I cry before the pain stops? What's the point of living?"

"How soon after you found your son's grave did you slip away yourself?"

"Oh, I don't know. Could be a year. They said I had 'consumption'; I stayed with my sister in Philadelphia 'til I died. My sister said I was consumed with grief. I'm buried up there in some lonely grave. But I come here to be with my Lenny, although I never seem to find him. Do you know where he is? Why isn't he here? I thought when I died that I would be able to come back here and find him."

And then another woman commented.

"Well at least you found your son's grave. I've been searching and searching to find my husband's grave, but I never found where they buried him. I'm tired of looking for him and I'm tired of grieving. I want closure. I want this pain to stop. Can you help me - please?"

Where Are Our Menfolk?

They all crowded around me, Abigail, Charlotte, Helen, Emma, Joanna, Leslie, Ashley and so many more mothers, sisters, daughters, wives, and fiancées. They were all looking for the men who never came home, never held them in their arms again, never sat down to the dinner table, never called their names again and never said goodbye.

All of these women came to find their beloved fallen soldiers. Some women had doggedly combed dozens of Civil War graveyards seeking that last thread of connection, that last glimmer of closure to put their hope to rest. Love never dies and whether or not any of them ever found their loved ones would never diminish how much they loved the men and boys who were never coming home.

"Where are our men if they aren't here by their graves? I thought after I died of pneumonia, that I would be able to be with my husband, but I can't find him!" Ashley seemed so bewildered.

"My name's Carol Ann Beck. Can you help me find Big Daddy? He went to war and never came back."

"I need to find my husband. He had blond hair, blue eyes, and a red beard. His name was Major Mitchell Pfeiffer, one of General Lee's boys gone to fight the Yankees."

"I've been looking for my husband, Zacharia. He was a Captain in the Union Army."

"My handsome husband, Reginald Putnam, was a sergeant in the Confederate Army. He was also a bugler. He loved to play that horn. I keep lookin' but I can't seem to find him anywhere. I'm Loretta, from Charleston, South Carolina. Whom did you lose? Who did you come looking for? Was your husband in the

Army? Was he a Yankee or a Rebel? When did you die?"

"Well, I didn't die," I said. "I've come to help all of you to crossover into the Heaven World. I frankly thought I would find Civil War soldiers here just like you all did and I'm a bit surprised to find each of you."

"Well, where are our menfolk? Why aren't they with you? If you've come to help us, did you help them too?"

"Ladies, I suspect that most of the men you are seeking do not realize that they have, in fact, died. Many of them are still fighting it out on battlefields all over the South. They were so intent on surviving the battle that they do not realize that the battle ended tragically for them. This means that they never saw their mortally wounded bodies lying there. Probably some of them never even felt the cannon blast or mine explosion that ended their lives. You will not find them here or at any other graveyard.

"I am baffled that you all seem to understand that you are each no longer in a mortal body. How did you realize that you died? How did you all decide to come to the gravesites of your loved ones?"

"I died of Scarlet Fever within two years of the war ending. As I was burning up with fever, I remember my momma saying 'Leslie, it's okay, you'll soon find Jesus and He'll reunite you and your husband, Theodore.' But when I left my body, I felt so angry! I didn't see Jesus and I didn't see Teddy either. I saw darkness, grayness and I came to the last place that I knew of where Teddy was camped. But he isn't here! I've been cheated! He never came home in life and now I can't even find him in death. It's so unfair. What good will crossing over do for any of us if our men are still on the battlefield?"

At this point I have filled the cemetery with tremendous light. The angelic escorts then reach out to each woman, offer them a beautiful honey-colored shawl for their grief-burdened shoulders. The women take them hesitantly. Abigail seems to speak for the group.

"I admit that I am feeling better. The bitterness of my grief is – is not quite as painful, but what about our men? Who will help them? I want to leave here so badly but I'm so unsure. I think we're all not sure we can leave our last link to our men . . . please understand, we want relief from this pain, but we can't abandon our soldiers."

"Once you have all crossed over, there will be tremendous comfort enveloping you. From your location in the Heaven World, you will be able to do far more for your men who never returned. Sometimes great assistance can be provided to those souls who do not realize that death has come upon them. These angels will guide you in the best way to help your men, your precious lost loves."

Epilogue

The methods of death for all of these women were so telling. Scarlet Fever is symbolically a 'raging' fever and the body turns this deep 'scarlet' color. War engenders an overwhelming volume of grief engulfing the person, hence death by 'consumption' or Tuberculosis. Pneumonia would have been a death by the lungs filling up with infection, again, the symbolism of drowning in the tidal wave of grief. Did their grief kill them by various methods? Listening to their stories, the volume of their pain overwhelmed their ability to continue living.

I directed the angels to assist these women in finding their lost loved ones as they crossed over into the Heaven World. Great service can be done for those souls trapped in the 4th dimension by those souls who have been released to the Heaven World. The prayers these women said for all of those years were not in vain. Help was given to each of them as well as to the men they lost, albeit in an indirect way.

Perhaps some of the thousands upon thousands of soldiers that my angelic teams have assisted in realizing that they have died, and to cross over into the Heaven World, will in fact be the loved ones that these grieving, tortured women so desperately seek. I pray with all my heart that this is true.

Those Southerners who survived the war were filled with anger and bitterness. General Sherman's philosophy of breaking the back of the South by burning his way from Atlanta to Savannah, left a huge swath of devastation in his path. Farms, plantations, cities, towns, and railroad stations were all torched. This action seared a smoldering fury among defeated Southerners.

There was also the peripheral grief of a country torn in half by war. Even though the North did not experience the personal devastation of having the battles fought in the states above the Mason/Dixon line that did not stop the energy of war from influencing every citizen of the North through the loss of fathers and sons, husbands, and brothers.

The Civil War brought heartache and desolation to families on both sides of this conflict. The wreckage of war seldom shows the deep emotional scars that families suffer for generation

The Indiana
Antique Mall

have always wondered about the level of hauntings in antique stores. As I answered a request for a remote view from the sister of a Navy buddy of mine, I realized I might find out. My friend's sister, Eleanor, and her cousin, Adele, own an antique store together, in a small town in Indiana.

Eleanor and Adele had experienced all kinds of episodes while owning this antique mall, but finally, when they read my first ghost book, Ghost Stories from the Ghosts' Point of View, Trilogy Vol. 1, they decided to contact me. When I spoke to them initially, they blurted out that all kinds of things were happening: objects moving, the usual doors closing by themselves, the 'feeling' that someone was there. I agreed to work on their place. I told them that I would call them in about a week.

But that week turned into two and finally, as I realized that three weeks had passed, I had to ask myself why I kept delaying this seemingly ordinary remote view. The only explanation I had was a persistent sense of dread, a deep feeling that I had no desire to see what I would find, not just in the store, but in the time before there was an antique store, an antique mall or modern civilization. Something else happened there, something extremely disturbing.

They Aren't Antiques to Them

As soon as I got there psychically, I was presented with all kinds of souls from all different stacks of time, all clinging to that which can never be taken with you upon death. Longing persists after death, including clinging to 'things' after passing.

Children are always confused at death and there she was, an adorable little five-year old girl baffled by the fact that her precious doll was no longer in her own bedroom at home. I had the vague impression that she was holding it when she died, which was why she was far more 'attached' to it than anyone would have suspected. Death is so lonely for children, and the doll was her only security; she was always going to be wherever that doll was. A current day person would readily have seen the doll move all by itself.

The next oblivious ghost was a very old woman, wearing a hand-tatted lace collar and a severe black dress with her hair up in a Gibson Girl type of bun. She was thoroughly polishing a 1920s mahogany dining room table - endlessly. It's possible she simply dropped from a heart attack or stroke while polishing it and never realized that she had passed away.

I watched a very elderly man jealously guard a diamond ring in a charming vintage setting. He had tears in his eyes because he could not understand why his beloved Clara was not still wearing the ring, he had given her. The last time he saw her, yesterday to him, it was still on her hand. How could it be in this place? How do you explain to any ghost that 'yesterday' could be 150 years ago?

An aged, very dignified lady, peacefully rocking in an old oak rocking chair seemed to be staring out a window. Her gray hair hung in crooked wisps that had escaped the severe bun she must have routinely worn. Her hands were weathered and wrinkled. She was no stranger to hard work. And it would have been the movement of that rocking chair that would have unnerved a customer seeking to purchase that possessed piece of furniture. Possession now takes on a new meaning.

A 'radio flyer' wagon with an adorable tow-headed little boy in it captured my attention next. He kept tugging on this obviously vintage red wagon so that he could go down that hill again – which was very likely what killed him. He looked to be around six or seven years old. His bloody shirt and the gash on his head were still clearly visible. Either he had no idea he died, or he found great comfort in sticking with his wagon, perennially lost in the moment of his death. His constant tugging on that wagon would have provided a 21st century observer with the visible movement of that wagon with no one present.

I was able to bring in teams of angels to help these souls as well as the hundreds of others inordinately attached to various objects. You may not be able to take it with you but that doesn't mean you release attachment to things when you die. Some souls haunt the object as some ghosts haunt people. There were at least 1,000 ghosts who needed help with their final transition in that store.

As the population of dead was cleared, the angels saw to them and offered them the comfort of the warmth of the light. The antique mall gradually vanished and revealed what that land looked like before there were people, shopping malls, highways, subdivisions, and telephone lines.

I'm so cold . . .

Now I see what appears to be an exceptionally cold winter. There are trees surrounding a snowy clearing. It is actively snowing as I watch this scene, as if I'm somehow transported back to that time and I am standing in the snow. I can feel the cold as if breathing it in would sting my warm, modern, California adjusted lungs. The dark leaden sky bodes more snow and a harshness that makes me feel deeply afraid, not so much for myself, but for whatever caused this swath of clearing that I can see.

I am so cold! It's 85 degrees outside my San Diego home and I'm freezing. I know I have to continue this remote view but there is a part of me that dreads it, is loath to see what is making me chilled to my core. I can feel the sadness coming on; a feeling of desolation sweeps over me. I have on jeans and a sweater and yet I cannot seem to get warm.

I stand there, in the penetrating cold, in another time and place, staring at this foreboding sky. Looking at rubble, I know that another image is about to materialize. Involuntarily I breathe in and the air feels emotionally cold. Living in two realms is so hard: to live in one and yet feel, sense, and know the other.

Finally, I see her, just one waif of a child in a thin shredded dress, standing there staring at the snow-covered rubble with her back to me. The bitter wind blows her long, brown pigtails that have escaped the sadly untied ribbon that did such a poor job of containing her beautiful chestnut hair. Where is her jacket? She must be freezing.

Before I speak to her, I study her a bit more. I don't believe she knows she's dead. She seems to be waiting for someone or something. I speak to her in the gentlest, softest voice. I don't wish to startle her, but there is no way to escape this: she's been alone for so long I doubt that there is any way to approach her without it seeming to be a surprise.

"I noticed you standing here in this brutal cold. May I offer you a wrap for your shoulders? Have you been waiting here long?"

She does not startle at all. She turned her head only slightly and glanced at me briefly. She continued to gaze back in the direction of her originally dedicated, focused stare.

"I'm waitin' for my pa to come git me." She states this flatly, without emotion, without acknowledgement of how odd this must have seemed. I continue to talk to her even though her back is to me.

"What's your name?"

"Ruth, Ruth Montgomery."

"How old are you, Ruth? What happened here?"

"I'm twelve. Best as I can tell, we done had a twister come through. I ain't never seen one. It come out of the night like some devil come to take us to hell. I was yellin' at Pa. Pa was yellin' at Ma. We tried to git them animals, but it come so fast, ain't nothin' to do. I'm waiting for Pa. He'll come back for me with Ma. I been waitin' a while. Uh, thank ya' kindly for this here blanket, ma'am."

This is a child of few words.

"What happened, Ruth, after the tornado? Did you survive it? Did you see your Pa afterward?"

Raw Horror

I asked this question gingerly because, as she turns all the way to speak to me, my stomach becomes instantly queasy. I can hardly look at the carnage done to her body. Ghosts present themselves to me at the final moment of their death. Whatever happened to them, whatever terrible indignity has been done to their body is what is visually presented to me. You think you'll get used to it; you think you can find that emotional anesthetic of detached compassion, but sometimes, the pure rawness of the horror done to a person leaves you speechless.

Ghost Stories from the Ghosts' Point of View

"After that twister took it all, I musta' got knocked out. Then I come to and looked for Ma and Pa, but I couldn't find 'em. I kept stumblin' on the mess that the twister left. The sound of the storm was still so loud as it was leavin', that I reckon' I couldn't hear it come 'til it was plumb on me. I turned to look for Pa in a different direction and there was a mountain lion. I guess that's what it was. It jumped right on me, but I fought it off. I fought like an old grizzly bear, scratchin' and punchin' that old mountain cat! I hit him so hard, he run away. I know Pa'll be proud of me for fightin' so hard. Then I got up and just kept waitin' for my Pa to come. Are you done asking me questions?"

This child had no idea that the mountain lion gutted her torso, leaving her insides hanging outside of her body. Some of her organs were strewn about. This was why her clothes were completely shredded. Her face was completely gone. Her neck was savagely severed all the way back to her spinal cord. There was no way this slip of a child fought off a mountain lion, which could have weighed as much as 265 pounds. I could not tell if she was dragged. I do suspect that the subconscious part of her left her body as soon as she saw the mountain lion but the conscious part of her believes that she successfully fought off a cougar.

There are situations when a soul knows on

a fundamental level that death is at hand, so the soul simply departs the body and does not feel the pain of the physical method of death. It is an effective vehicle of emotional self-preservation to handle leaving the body. The soul will need tremendous healing in the Divine realms, something this sweet soul will not ever find waiting in this desperately icy evening in Indiana.

"Ruth, would you like some help finding your pa?"

"Well, I reckon I would. Do ya' know where he be? Can you git me to him?"

I had sent my team to seek out Ruth's parents who, as it naturally turns out, were also looking for her. I created a campfire and piled blankets around it and invited them all to come and warm themselves from the relentless cold of death. Other souls who died by the misfortunes of the twister joined them. Eventually we had quite a group of people. I asked them what year this was. They said it was 1850 and were baffled as to why I would ask such an odd, obvious question.

When Ruth saw her parents, especially her father, she ran to him using the body she thought she had. She hugged him with her entire body, jumping into his arms.

"Look Pa, I fought off a mountain cat! He come right at me, but I bit and scratched and punched him and then he run off. Weren't I brave Pa? Aren't you proud of me? See I waited right here for you. I'm so glad to see ya' Pa. It seems so long."

"Ah Ruth, your Ma and me are real proud of you for being such a right brave girl. Oh honey, we missed you so much!"

Her father was missing an arm, but he hugged her with the arms he thought he had. Her mother was bloody. But in death, in the mysterious environs of the 4th dimension, none of the physical traumas matter. Each person saw his or her loved one, whole, perfect, and healthy. Whenever we are reunited with our loved ones, the love within us begins to satisfy the longing, and starts to heal the cruel wounds of mortal life.

The reunion of friends and neighbors, families and pets was so powerful, so joyful that none of them noticed that the campfire slowly disappeared, and they were all being gently guided into the compassionate light that is the Divine.

Epilogue

Once this scene terminated, I stepped back into the slipstream of time and searched the past in that spot of land. But there were no more ghosts to be found here.

The owners noted that the unnerving paranormal activity in their shop had ceased and their business felt calm now. They were most curious about who was there and whether or not they should be fearful of antiques with ghosts in tow, in the future.

I explained that their antique mall was cleared for as long as it takes the owners to bring in a new piece with a ghostly guardian attached. Antique stores are always haunted because the old items are saturated with the predecessor energy of any and all previous owners. Predecessor energy is so powerful in some situations, that one object can negatively or positively affect a new owner's life through the energy being emitted by the item.

This is especially true of jewelry because certain pieces would have been worn every day. The shop owners will seldom know what happened to the previous item holders, including whether or not the person was murdered or died a terrible death while wearing the item, or whether or not the object was used in a violent way.

My clients were quiet for a moment and then wondered how they could protect themselves and their antique stock from the effects of this predecessor energy.

I suggested to Eleanor and Adele, that they say The Crossing Over Prayer© each day. This prayer is a tool to remove fear and mystery from the concept of having ghosts around. If they are able to say the prayer daily, then no matter what 'possessed' antique item comes in, these owners will be able to help that soul find the light, which is truly a Divine service.

Big Willie

My call from a previous client surprised me.

"Hey Tina, I've got this weird thing happening with my dog, Chester. He keeps sniffing and pawing at a corner of my bedroom. Now and then he barks to get my attention. He looks at me and he looks at the corner. I know I'm supposed to get it, but the dog baffles me. Look, this is a new house, we've barely been here six months, so we don't have termites or bees, although I did have that area checked out just in case some insect found its way in here. I don't want to think that this place is haunted, but maybe it is. I don't know. You need to look and tell me what's wrong with my dog or hell, I don't know maybe it's my house again."

"Do you have any other clues that this could be paranormal?"

"No, just the dog driving me nuts worrying about this corner. I don't sense anything, don't hear anything, no weird dreams, no smells, nothing."

"Alright then, I'll get to work."

Robert's new home was only a couple of blocks from the beach. His front yard still had the look of new landscape imbedded into the white sand of his front yard. The old growth trees were carefully kept, and new palm trees were planted nearby. His modern 3,000 square foot house with large windows seemed the antithesis of any type of ghostly dwelling but then I have learned that new homes can be just as haunted as older homes. Predecessor energy attaches to a location as well as to a house. His creamy white siding and bright geraniums on the front steps presented a clean modern look. Nothing eerie or scary about this house; it looked like a gorgeous, happy place to live.

Robert has previous experience with ghosts and the paranormal, so his call was not unusual. With this client, I have no idea what I will find, especially since I have now been to his Virginia Beach home twice before, and now to this new one. Time to see what was there.

The Psychic Dog

Most animals can see not only in this mortal 3rd dimension but also in the 4th dimension. The problem for animals is that their owners have no idea how to communicate with their pets or understand that they are identifying a potential problem. Luckily, Robert is different. He sensed immediately that his dog was telling him that he had some type of psychic problem.

This was my first remote view of Robert's new home. The clean, modern feeling I sensed from the outside continued throughout the house. The beautiful wood floors, the fresh, bright feeling in the décor throughout the home did not appear to be hiding any lost souls. So far, nothing in that entire house could be found, nothing, until I came to Robert's bedroom.

There was Chester, sitting there, almost as if he were waiting for me to arrive and help him with the group of souls who were just standing there politely waiting for something. He seemed to be guarding them, not because they were dangerous, but because he was trying to tell someone that these men and women were standing there.

His Name was Big Willie

A group of former slaves had entered Robert's house. The spokesman for the group was an enormous man by the name of Big Willie. He was just one among many men who were there to give 'Dr. Jim' a message. I already knew that Robert had been a doctor in a previous life during the Civil War. However, I had no idea what his connection was with these former slaves. Each man was trying to speak to him, to give him an important message, but it was Big Willie who ended up doing all of the talking to me.

"Hi there Ma'am. I's Big Willie an I come here to talk ta' Dr. Jim. We's all concerned for him. He keeps thinkin' about killin' hisself an' we all been tryin' to talk him outta doin' that."

"Well, Big Willie, I'm pleased to meet you and I'm deeply touched that you and the others are so concerned for Robert or as you knew him, Dr. Jim. How do you know he plans to take his own life?"

"'Cause we hear him thinkin' about how he hates this here life and that it'd be better iffin' he just weren't here no more."

"Can you tell me how you know him?"

"Sure, Light Lady, I'll tells ya'. We's been 'memberin' long ago when he was caring for us on them plantations. He was kind. He don't never mind that we's slaves. Ta' him we's just people who be a needin' hep'. We all memba' him. Sees all a us astandin' here? I's a talkin' for dem all. Can you help him ta' know what we's a sayin'?"

"Of course, I'll tell him. Please continue."

It seemed to me that talking was almost difficult for Big Willie. He seemed acutely conscious of his inability to be articulate. His discomfort was obvious. Ordinarily he was a shy man; speaking for this group seemed almost embarrassing to him. However, because he was such a caring soul, he was able to move past his awkwardness and tell me what he wanted to share.

"We wants him ta' know that even though he's real sad at how life's a treatin' him and how sad it is that folks die, that each lil' thing he does makes a difference. His kindness an' his carin' means everythin' ta all a us."

"I'm sure he has no idea how you all feel. I'm happy to tell him, to help him to know that his being here matters so much and how his help for all of you mattered in that time awhile back when you were on the plantations.

"Big Willie, do you know why I'm here? Do you understand that I have come to help you move on into that light you see over there?"

I had already begun to have my team of Angels of Transition assemble to help these gentlemen to cross over. The light was now readily visible for them.

"We know'd it, ma'am. We did. We just be wantin' him to get that we wants ta' return the help he done give ta' us before we moves on."

The defining moments in a person's life are not always the big events, but often the little expressions of kindness that are a matter of course for most people. However, for a former slave, any act of kindness was a treasured memory. Slavery ripped out a man's soul. It destroyed the thought of family, of the love of children, and of the tenderness of the daily elements of normal living. Existing as a slave was never a normal life. It was a life interrupted or a life never fully started. Bondage was immediate upon birth in this new world if you were a slave.

Robert, or as they knew him in that past life, Dr. Jim, was a country doctor to the wealthy plantation owners. However, he also doctored the slaves that made those huge farms work. Dr. Jim's kindness lifted each slave up to a level of dignity they had seldom experienced. He helped them to mitigate the feelings of oppression they felt in their lives, even, if for only a few moments. Robert's tenderness with their illnesses and injuries helped to shift something inside of them because they died without as much bitterness as they might have had. They died in a place of hope because of his compassion for their situation despite suffering unspeakable brutality.

Yet, Robert must have felt like he had so little to give them during that time. Once the Civil War started, Robert became a Union Army surgeon. Supplies became limited as the war progressed, which meant that there was absolutely nothing left to treat sick and injured slaves. What little Robert had as a surgeon, was given over to the Union Army to help their wounded men and/or Confederate prisoners of war.

". . . healing, isn't always about bandages and medicine . . ."

Healing isn't always about bandages and medicine, hospitals, and procedures. Healing is sometimes more about helping a soul to progress because of your kindness, your compassion, and your insight into the dignity due every human being. This is the true healing that Dr. Jim gave men like Big Willie all those years ago. They wanted him to know in their own humble way that he made a huge difference for them. They felt that they owed him a debt of gratitude, a debt that they now wanted to repay.

"Can you tell him that we been wantin' him to believe in his goodness an not kill hisself in this life he's 'alivin'? When he heped us, we'd plum give up hope they be any goodness left in any white man, in this whole world."

Willie went on to say that when Robert cared for their injuries, same as he would have provided for any white man, that action gave them a feeling of dignity. And even though they still died, even though he couldn't save them physically, he lifted them out of the sheer volume of sadness they had encountered in that brutal lifetime. They found love in their hearts, and this saved them; it elevated them. His act of compassion to them was the greatest gift they had ever received, and they wanted to return that compassion to him in this life.

"Big Willie, why didn't you and all your companions move on since Dr. Jim had helped you so much? Did the light come for you?"

"I don't rightly know. I reckon we was waitin' for Dr. Jim, and when we found him here at this place, we wanted to hep him. Will you hep him? Light Lady, tell Dr. Jim ta' live life, live 'cause he matters and 'cause he's a makin' a difference. He done made a difference in our world and now he's a makin' a difference in this here world."

Big Willie wiped a tear away as he nervously fingered his tattered old brown hat. The men behind him nodded silently in agreement. I assured him that I would do exactly as they had requested.

Once Big Willie had said his peace, he seemed more than ready to head into the light. I saw the biggest, broadest smile grace his generous features when his angel placed the Divine coat around him. He stood a bit straighter, walked a bit taller and showed the true dignity of his soul. I watched as the energy of the angels and the Divine coat began to heal the deep emotional and physical wounds that slavery created within him. Big Willie had experienced unspeakable cruelty as well as acts of quiet kindness. He had been a witness to the wreckage caused by the Civil War and its devastating aftermath.

Once they had crossed over, they were slaves no longer. Joy graced their lined faces. As the light embraced each of them, the shackles of fear, humiliation, intimidation, and loneliness slipped away. Friends and family greeted them, welcomed them, and led them into hope and happiness. Finally, their suffering was over, and they were home.

Changing Your View of the World

Once all of the men had transitioned, I sealed up the spiritual hole and cleaned and cleared the house. Robert's dog stopped pawing endlessly at the corner of the bedroom, trying to show him those ghosts. There were no more ghosts coming into the house.

I had a very long talk with Robert about his view of life. He had no idea that these men were in his house much less that he had ever had contact with them. He was ashamed to admit that he had long considered leaving and had pondered how he would kill himself. Since he had never shared this information with anyone, there would be no way for me to have known, had Big Willie not heard Robert's thoughts, and enlightened me.

"Robert, I urge you to consider how important it is for men like Big Willie and his fellow slaves that you continue living, really living. The staggering nightmare that was the Civil War is directly influencing your feelings of hopelessness today. When the trauma of a past life is this intense, when you were trying desperately to help people to live through staggering injuries, and disease without adequate equipment, medicines or supplies you may have felt like a terrible failure. The truth is that now, just as you did then you're helping people with your medical skills. Only in this life, you have far more tools. I know that you don't often feel that you are making a difference, but that measure is going to be unique for each person."

"Don't you see the horrible things people are still doing to each other, to their own bodies? There are still wars! When does it end? I admit it: I'm often filled with a feeling of hopelessness with what I see. Man's endless inhumanity to man does not seem to have changed very much since the Civil War."

"No effort given in love and kindness is ever wasted: it's all important. Don't you see? You matter, Robert, to both the living and the dead."

Robert's eyes filled with tears, and he

began to choke up as he acknowledged these feelings. Then he was silent for a moment. Finally, he took a deep breath and as he began to speak again, he was different.

"I've been so angry! I go from frustration to despair. I admit that sometimes I have wondered if it was all worth it. Look, I'll try. I know that I can't let the cruelty of some destroy the good I can do for the people I can help. I can't believe it took a ghost to tell me this."

I have no doubt that when it is Robert's natural time to cross over, there will be quite a reception committee waiting for him. I feel honored to know such a fine soul. I felt privileged to have met Big Willie and his companions. Even the best among us get down now and then. The critical element is to remember our goodness. What we are doing matters on so many levels and in so many dimensions and we may never truly know how our good work will have helped someone. We have to trust that the energy of goodness and kindness will echo out beyond time.

Epilogue

The looming question is how could ghosts who died in the 1860s find someone in the 21st century?

I have long pondered this issue. Most ghosts have no idea that they have died. Most ghosts simply continue to exist where they perished not realizing the end has come. But in this highly unusual case, these ghosts not only knew they had died, but they were also aware of who helped them while they were alive. They also knew how to stay connected to a person through the stacks of time and space.

The only explanation is that in some unusual circumstances, souls know how to find each other. It could be that the aka cord connections that exist between human beings continue after death. Because these men had been slaves in that lifetime, the trauma of their life kept their frequency lowered preventing them from transitioning to the Heaven World. When Robert reincarnated and lived somewhere near where they had lived and died, these men reconnected. Thousands of Civil War dead reconnected to this one person repeatedly, so seeing these slaves from that time was not unusual.

Does proximity to that past energy matter? Not necessarily. A person can live in another part of the country or even half a world away and still be connected to a past event in another time and place. Time and distance do not matter in the 4th dimension.

Just because a person dies does not mean that the energy that he or she expended in one life is forever gone, lost, frozen. The energy of who we are, what we did and how we treated other people lingers in locations. It binds us karmically to times and places and to souls.

I often find myself deeply moved by the love and compassion of human beings living and dead. Some souls are so profoundly filled with love for another person, that they lift themselves up and out of the horror in which many have found themselves. And such is the case here.

We are just beginning to scratch the surface of understanding how life and death work. How the energy of a mortal soul moves in and among the lives of others. We are also beginning to understand how the interconnections of our actions affect so many people over time.

Update:

Robert did eventually take his life despite reassurances to him that he mattered. When his family called me, I immediately crossed him over.

Some souls simply cannot find peace and their method of passing will never be ours to judge.

The Fort Story Colonists

n June of 2012, I was in Virginia Beach, Virginia to celebrate my niece's high school graduation. It was a most hectic time and we were overwhelmed with all of the graduation events. Finally, everything was over, and we went out to lunch at the beach. We were having a great time and after lunch we decided to visit Fort Story and the First Landing at the Cape Henry Memorial.

Fort Story is an Army base founded in 1914. There is a lovely spot near the vertically black and white stripped Old Cape Henry lighthouse (built in 1791), where a wooden walkway leads you to a striking bluff that overlooks the beach. The elevated, grey, wooden plank walkway is beautiful, weathered and worn. This path winds you up an incline, past all the tangled old growth plants with spiky looking vines, which are oddly matched with the beauty of the humble morning glory vines and the warm, familiar fragrance of native honeysuckle. The mesh of the vines seems to have bound them together as a protection from the relentless wind of this promontory.

The top of the path surprises you with the stunning, sheer intensity of the salty sea spray of the cool Atlantic Ocean as it hits your face when you take that last step to the top. Then the view up and down this beach further steals your breath away. I have stood here many times and pictured the first European ships that anchored out and sought the imagined riches of this new America, this New World. Few of them had any idea that the riches they sought were not the obvious ones of gold and silver but the character traits that would be required to live in such a challenging land.

This specific area is also part of the National Park Service. There is a plaque there that explains that this exact view of the Chesapeake Bay was where, in 1781, 24 French Galleons held off the supplies and reinforcements coming in for General Cornwallis' troops during the end of the Revolutionary War. A huge battle ensued, and the French held the line. A few days later General Cornwallis surrendered at Yorktown and the Revolutionary War was over.

But I had no sense of any ghosts there that day, wandering the empty beach.

We read all the National Park Service information and then wound our way slowly through the densely wooded park to head back to my sister's house. As we were passing some of the older parts of the army base and park, I began to notice that I had an odd feeling begin to come over me. I began coughing almost uncontrollably, a sure sign that someone is trying to get my attention. My sister pulled over.

I became very still and began to look into the ether of this location, down the road that we had just traveled. There they were, three desperate ghosts, seeking someone to listen to them.

"Please help us, it's so cold here."

"Please, can you see us? Please help us, it's so cold here."

"Yes," I replied, "I can see you and what also looks like two other men. Who are you? Where did you come from?"

"I'm Eleanor and this is my husband, Charles. Charles Wolden. This is our friend Philip. We were traveling together to another encampment and we stopped for the night and it's as if we never 'woke up.' The light of day never comes. We don't understand. There are all these terrifying little animal-like creatures that keep coming at us, tormenting us. Sometimes it feels as if we are all in hell."

Her telltale comment that the 'light of day never comes' tells me that she died at night. This is why the light of day can never come for any of them. The 'terrifying little animal-like creatures' that she described are something called Lower Realm Intelligences. Roughly four feet high, inky black with red eyes, these beings are often called little torturers because they exist only in the 4th dimension and mercilessly harass those who have died a violent death.

Eleanor looked to be about forty, but then she could have been much younger; women all of those years ago aged rapidly under such harsh conditions.

"I think I can help you. Can you tell me what year it is? Do you know?"

"We are so grateful that you can hear us and see us. It has been so dark here and we don't know how long we've been here. The year is – I'm not sure what the year is. The days have all run together, but I believe it's 1640. Life's so hard here. I had no idea that it would be so difficult to live here."

"What are you doing on this road?"

"Road? We only see a pathway. Philip over there is from the other encampment north of us, about two days away. There're some very sick colonists there and Philip was sent to our settlement to fetch me, and my bag of herbs. There are so few of us who know what to use for healing. Herbs, tree bark, roots and leaves can heal you or poison you. The Indians originally taught us what was safe to use, but not all the Indians liked us being here. Eventually, they retreated to other areas and we did not see much of them. The fact was that many of the natives here were split in their belief that we should even share the land with them. There has been violence. One of the settlers in another encampment was killed. I – I was so terrified to make this trip. We hoped that if Philip made it here that we might make it back to help those sick people. I guess I'm not quite sure exactly what happened to us."

"Why is your husband with you, why didn't you and Philip simply go to that other encampment?"

"Well, it isn't proper for a married woman and another man to be traveling alone for so many days. We wished one of us could stay back with our children, but Charles had to come protect my honor. Besides, we all felt, I mean the group of us felt that we would be safer if there were three of us."

"You look so chilled, is it wintertime?"

"Yes, this is my fifth winter here and I have never known winters so numbingly cold. It's horrible. I am wearing every single piece of clothing I own and I'm still freezing. We have so few pieces of cloth to make clothes and the days are so bitter and long that we have to wear piles of clothing to make it through the days and the terrible nights. We spent the night here because it's freezing, we were exhausted and it's too far to walk in one day. We wanted to do it in one day, but the snow and the chill took their toll on us. I couldn't go any farther and we stopped to rest, eat, and sleep. We were going to break camp at first light, but it never gets light, it just stays dark.

"I can't really see anything. I – I guess, I guess we're dead if you can see us and talk to us. You are the first person I've seen and you're real bright, a bright type of light almost. I can't see anyone else, and I don't understand why I feel like I'm in such a dark place. The Bible didn't prepare us for this type of death, but I don't quite know how we died. Do you know? Can you tell what happened to us?"

Gathering Emotional Courage

An agonizing argument plays out in my head. Would I want to know the raw truth of what happened to me? Would I want to know? The knowing changes everything. Maybe they think they froze to death. Would it be kinder to let them think this or to understand that freezing to death would have been a much kinder, less violent death? What is the kindest action? What is the greatest good? If nothing more can happen to them now, if they will learn this anyway once they are in the Heaven World, then what's the difference? Their life just lived will be reviewed, so that they can learn from the experience. Besides they are owed the truth as it was shown to me. Even though they cannot see it, I can clearly see the entire scenario.

I gathered my emotional courage and simply explained it as plainly as I could.

"You were all murdered in your sleep by three natives who tracked you all day long. They waited until you went to sleep and then they attacked you. But not one by one: this was a planned coordinated attack. One native person was assigned to each of you and your bodies were hacked to death with a tomahawk at the same staggering moment.

"You would never have seen it coming or, mercifully, felt it as it was happening. With one tremendous blow, the blade of each tomahawk was imbedded in each of your hearts. It was not an accidental blow: it was a deliberate thrust into the very core of your being. The first wound was designed to cut your hearts out and then to cut your heart into two parts. Then, as difficult as it is to explain this, each native did even more than this, butchering every single organ in your body.

The native people of this time believed that if these body parts were so destroyed, each of you could not cross over into the Heaven World and could never return to their land.

"The Native Americans wanted to be rid of the white man, his families, and his ways. They thought that if they destroyed the very essence of each of you by cutting up your hearts and other organs that you could never find peace in the afterlife and never again return to this land. Their method of death for each of you was planned and executed to create the maximum amount of carnage to your exhausted bodies. I'm – I'm so sorry."

Eleanor, Charles, and Phillip are speechless. But then Charles and Philip never said anything anyway. They all stand together in stunned silence. Perhaps it is a small blessing that none of them can actually see their butchered bodies. This is surely too staggering to absorb.

They are horrified and astonished to learn the gruesome details of their individual deaths. Eleanor angrily wants to know why no one prepared her for this or any other kind of death.

"Why doesn't the Bible prepare us for death beyond seeking God? We've been here searching this dark place for we don't know how long. We finally realized we had died, but nothing prepared us for this. How could this happen to us? We worked so hard! We're good Christian people. This isn't supposed to happen to us!" [I can feel her anger increasing.] "This is horrible! This means that our families, our friends must have eventually found our mutilated bodies. I hope no one told our children. Who took our children? What happened to the settlers we were supposed to help?"

I felt Eleanor's anger and frustration at the struggles she encountered simply spill out.

"We tried so hard to be friends to the Indians, teach them our ways and learn their ways so that we could survive, but obviously they never fully trusted us. I guess we are taking their land . . . but there is so much land, surely, there is plenty for us all. I just can't believe that this has happened to us."

These murders were designed to be a deterrent. But the Indians did more to these people. They wanted a trophy of their kill and Eleanor's hair was a soft and electric red, exceptionally long and beautiful. Charles and Philip both had light blond hair, long as men wore their hair at that time. This thick hair was also insulating around a person's neck against the penetrating cold. Their bodies were not only butchered beyond recognition, but they were also scalped. I wondered about what their clothing looked like originally. I could not make out what they were wearing because their clothes were completely soaked in blood; their body essence was a butchered mass of flesh, organs, and bone.

The perpetuation of that feeling of spiritual abandonment exacerbated their sense of emotional isolation. I made sure that these three souls could feel the healing warmth coming from the Divine embrace of the glowing blankets brought to them by the angels. These blankets help to restore the very essence of their souls so that their decimated spiritual frequencies could begin to rise to a level that will enable them to take those critically important steps to that crossover point.

"Maybe I knew we were dead. We kept hoping that the dawn would eventually come, but until now, it's only been dark. It's almost a sooty darkness, and then, as I said, these beings we don't recognize that seem to come at us in these terrifying moments but yet we can never fully see them . . . it's torture. I can't describe it. I'm so tired, so confused."

Eleanor is quiet for a moment. Then she continued in a voice barely above a whisper, the full impact of her grief just beginning to seep into the quiet recesses of her shattered heart.

"We never got to see our children again. The people in the other settlement probably died and now I don't know what has happened to all of them. I don't understand. Why would God let this happen to us? We came for a better life. We came with the Good Book, to teach the gospel to the heathen. How could this happen? I don't . . . I don't want to see my body . . . "

She turns away. Her husband and Philip bow their heads. I could not tell if this was from relief or grief or perhaps a bit of both.

"It isn't necessary for any of you to see your body. It's also not something that I can explain, why you all died. It's what happened in that time. All you need to see is the angel standing beside each of you who will guide you all into the Heaven World. When you are feeling better, when the light and warmth of that healing has penetrated your very being, then we can begin to help each of you to cross over. Tell me, how you are feeling?"

"We're confused, afraid, but we are feeling warmer and maybe that's enough for us now. I'm ready. Maybe we can see our parents whom we left in England. Maybe they will be there for us. I – I want to see our children. They would surely have thought we abandoned them, or that . . . or that we died."

She simply does not understand how long she has been dead, and that she may also find her children in the Heaven World when she crosses over.

I nod to the angels and they gently guide

them all into that healing light, that place of hope, rebirth, and renewal: The Heaven World. However, these three may find that they need an exceptionally long time in that healing light of heaven, so that the energy of their soul essence can once again be restored before they can return to the challenges of life on earth.

Epilogue

Eleanor's sense of confusion during their endless time in the 4th dimensional darkness, having to face those terrifying 'dark beings' or Lower Realm Intelligences that haunted and terrified them, was towering. Because she felt betrayed by her faith, her frequency plummeted from her sense of despair and the sheer violence of her method of death. So many things conspired for these poor souls to be in that spot of earth for 382 years. Even though time did not exist for Eleanor and her companions, there is a part of them that does feel, on some level, that loss of time, as if a deep weariness sets in, a need for the ordeal to finally be over.

Very, very few faiths tell anyone what to do at death, what to expect at death and how to understand the many things that can happen to a soul once he or she exits the corporal body and transitions automatically to the 4th dimension. Only the 23rd Psalm offers us a glimpse of the 4th dimension and the need to ask God to be with us. Yet even this famous Psalm does not *directly* encourage a soul to request an angel to help them. Some faiths even feign ignorance of angels or the help that can be provided by these ambassadors from God.

The critical importance of assisting souls to cross over cannot be overstated. Trauma itself makes crossing over automatically challenging because it lowers frequency. The more severe the trauma, the lower the soul frequency becomes. Exacerbating the situation is the critical element that the soul is never completely sure that he or she has died because they cannot see their own body after a severe trauma. Sadly, this is why so much help was required for these souls and the same is going to be true for any soul in any traumatic situation.

The cruel irony is that these supposed 'primitive' Native Americans understood this. They deliberately did things to the bodies of each of these colonists that would preclude that person's transition to the Heaven World. The Native Americans were far savvier about life after death, frequency and imprisoning a soul than any white settler could have imagined. While they may not have specifically understood the frequency issue, they seemed to have an understanding of the power of ending the life of an enemy with a traumatic act.

It would be easy to judge the Native American actions as savage. However, perhaps we would be wise to ask ourselves how readily we would embrace any intruder who simply took all of our property and then expected us to accept this action with a smile on our faces. Imagine those same people telling us that there is so much that surely, we would be willing to share all that we have to people who never asked our permission, never showed gratitude and who never took care of the very land that they so often ruthlessly took.

History tells us that many Native Americans tribes did try to come to some accommodation with the white man, but they were met with only marginal success. Sometimes, progress comes at a terrible price.

Surrender Field

I t's a beautiful, open, seemingly empty field. There are no trees on it now, only honey-colored wild grasses gently swaying in the warm June breeze. The ordinariness of the grasses, offer no visible clue that this acre of land symbolized the beginning of a bright future for our country and the end to a bloody war for independence. There are tremendous pine trees that ring this quiet, empty battlefield, standing as silent woody witnesses to another chapter of man's inhumanity to man, mitigated solely by a moment of sanity when war came to a blessed and abrupt end.

Surrender Field is located in Yorktown, Virginia. It's the sight of General Charles Cornwallis' surrender of 8,000 English troops to General George Washington, on October 19, 1781. This action successfully ended the eight years of the Revolutionary War, and effectively changed the entire world forever. I would imagine that General Cornwallis could not conceive of defeat. He fully expected English Admiral Thomas Graves to run the French blockade off of the Virginia coast. But Graves lost the Battle of the Virginia Capes, thereby denying Cornwallis any hope of reinforcements and supplies. It was over.

But Surrender Field is not empty: the anger and frustration of the English, and the joy and relief of the Continental Army still linger. The ghosts of soldiers past are still active there, waiting. Waiting for word that for them, for their situation, the war can finally be over.

Silent Witness

One of the 'silent witnesses' ringing the field was a tremendously old pine tree; its strong trunk so wide that two people could not wrap their arms around it. As I walked over to touch the tree, to get a sense of the land and the area, I gingerly stepped past the lush poison ivy and the persistent anthills. Once I was able to lay my hand on this noble pine, I realized that this tree had become a type of spiritual 'antenna' whereby I could readily connect with the past. I was instantly startled by the fact that I could immediately hear him complaining, bitterly, as if the stupidity of his situation was eternally haunting him.

"That pompous ass! Why doesn't he surrender? There's no place to go! Admiral Graves isn't coming with supplies! The French have cut him off. We're doomed. Why's he holding out? How many of us have to die for His Lordship's vanity? Why can't he just admit

228

defeat? We lost the bloody battle! We're going to lose the bloody war and General Cornwallis is too stupid to see it!

"Here we are, standing in neat rows while the Continentals just pick us off. How senseless is this type of fighting? The French, the Indians and the Continentals don't fight this way. They have a better way."

"What's your name and position, soldier?"

"I'm Private Mitchell, an unwilling soldier in General Cornwallis' army from hell. Why doesn't he surrender? I keep saying it over and over, why? Why are we all standing here getting picked off? Can't he see what's happening? It's just a matter of time before I die, before we all die. How many of us have to die for His Lordship to figure it out?"

"Why didn't you desert? Why didn't you join the Continentals? Did you think about that?"

"Of course, I thought about it! I wanted to leave so badly, I was just afraid that the Continentals would think I was a spy and return me to Cornwallis and then I would be shot as a deserter. What choice did I have? Who are you anyway? What's a woman doing here in the middle of the battle?"

"I'm here to help you, here to let you know that the war is over. Cornwallis did surrender. However, you never got to see this momentous event."

"The way you're talking, your Ladyship, sounds like I died. Maybe I was too bloody angry to realize I died. How can I even see my own blood on these 'bloody' red coats they put us in? How were we expected to survive when the Continentals could shoot us like sitting ducks from trees, from behind rocks? They had cover. We were still marching about in perfect rows in our brilliant red coats. We never learned how to fight in this savage new world. Even the French fought better than the English. I wish I could have joined them, the Continentals, to help them defeat his Lordship."

Private Mitchell looks down at his red coat and sees a slow trickle of blood as he finally acknowledges the tiny death round that penetrated his bright red uniform through to his heart. Death would have been instantaneous. He very probably never had any idea that he was hit. There are between 600-800 ghostly English soldiers in this field endlessly fighting the Continentals and fervently hoping that this war would be over so that they can either return to England or start a new life here.

"Guess I died didn't I. Damn! I never got to see the end! So, His Lordship finally surrendered? Look at how many of us had to die! Look at this butchery! The Continentals and the French overwhelmed us and still he waited and waited. Day after day, all this time we've been waiting for him to surrender. So, when we died that day, or it feels like night, that moment just continued? None of us ever saw the sun again. General Washington routed His Lordship, did he? General Cornwallis had to face surrender? You have to tell me. How did it end?"

"Cornwallis realized, just as you said, that Admiral Graves was never coming with supplies or reinforcements. He must have accepted that with the combined forces of the Continentals and the French, that General Washington had finally outmaneuvered him. He realized that there was no further battle left to fight. He did ultimately agree to surrender on October 17th, but the official surrender ceremony took place on October 19th because Cornwallis feigned being 'indisposed.' He had his second in command, Brigadier General Charles O'Hara offer General Cornwallis' sword of surrender. General Washington's second in command Major General Benjamin Lincoln accepted Cornwallis' sword. The English band even played the song: 'The World Turned Upside Down' during the formal surrender."

"This was totally humiliating! Cowardly Cornwallis! The greatest army defeated by a bunch of farmers and the French for God's sake! How could Cornwallis let this happen? If he knew it was inevitable, why did he wait so long? What an idiot! I realize that I must be dead because speaking like this if I was alive would have put me in front of a bloody firing squad.

"My day keeps beginning over and over and the Continentals keep coming at us and we have no place to go. I can see that we are lined up like sitting ducks. Blood comes . . . out of my red coat. It stings a little. I couldn't be sure; my coat was already the color of blood. I understand now. As I turn, I can now see my body; I see other soldiers standing by their bodies, too. What a waste. I should've left the Army a long time ago. When will this all be over? Is it over now? Is that why you're here?"

"Yes, I'm here to offer you a bit of warmth for your weary body. Can you feel this warm cloak embrace your tired shoulders? Can you feel the light it emits penetrate deep within you?"

"Yes - yes I can."

He responds woodenly, almost as if he is numb from the whole experience. I look out across the entire field of soldiers: English, French and Continentals finally being embraced by this light of the Divine. One of the angels nods that they are ready for their weary charges to make their final journey.

Private Mitchell did not look back. His shoulders hunched over in defeat and his slow, plodding gait told me how depressed he had become as a soul. When he stepped upon the light bridge, the penetrating essence of that light began to shift the energy of his soul as he joined his comrades in the blaze of light that is the Divine.

Epilogue

The ghosts I initially saw were still fighting, still praying for that agonizing day to finally be over, and still hoping for a miracle. The arrival of the crossing over light was the answer to their unspoken prayers.

Assisting the dead is a miracle for these soldiers. Some of them never imagine that help can come. If you happen to visit a national battlefield, say The Crossing Over Prayer© at the end of this book to offer assistance to all those souls who may have no idea that they have died, who have no conception that what they think they are feeling is all a tragic illusion. This humble service is the essence of Light Work; it is the heart of compassion and is truly, the hope of salvation.

Perhaps the trees that hold the energy of battle can be relieved, to a degree, of their burden. I am ever grateful for the patient pine tree that enabled me to connect with Private Mitchell.

Caol, Scotland

Just a Bit of House Cleaning

I get requests all the time to clear houses. Sometimes it is simply routine: a family buys a house, and they want it cleared, or someone's renter leaves and they want that person, or couple's energy removed. Often, it is a store that wants the energy of a previous business cleared. I have even had schoolteachers request that a classroom be cleared after a particularly difficult school year ended.

Sometimes I feel more like a psychic cleaning/clearing lady than anything more special than that. But then I remember that for the souls that find the light, my 'cleaning and clearing' sweeps away the darkness many of them have been experiencing over time. It also helps homeowners and renters to feel like they have made a spiritual difference.

There is another facet to this: removing the

dead helps the earth to be a bit less burdened by those souls whose darkness depresses the etheric structure of the planet. Consider how toxic a battlefield would be. Graveyards are never kind to the ground that must play host to the energy of a dead soul.

The call that came in to clear a space after a renter left, should have been routine. I had worked on this home some time before. The request this time was only to clear the room where the renter had been living. The homeowner said the energy felt strangely 'heavy' after she left, and he wanted that space to feel as great as the rest of the home felt.

My client thought he was merely requesting a psychic cleansing after his renter left, but neither he nor I could have guessed how this simple request for clearing her energy would change our perception of time and space.

How Can This Be?

I began as I always do, scoping out the property on Google Earth. I typed in the address and selected the correct location for my client. But I noticed something odd: the street name and house number in California were identical to a property in Caol, Scotland (Great Britain). There are no coincidences; I had no idea what this could mean.

I began scanning and clearing the entire current house in Santa Barbara, California. The house seemed to be in good shape. The previous clearing was still very much intact. However, the homeowner was right, the area where his renter was living had a very unusual feeling. I moved on any negative or questionable energy, but I could immediately tell that there was much more to see. I had a sense I was being pulled way back in time. Now I've slipped back to not just another time, but a completely different location on Earth. No idea what would be unfolding. How could a location in California connect me to a location halfway around the world?

I could not tell you precisely what year it was only that it was in 'Olde' Scotland. It could be as far back as Shakespeare's time, the time of Queen Elizabeth I. It could be the late 1500s or early 1600s. It was the era of great seafarers, brave men who made the perilous trek between the New World and England, hoping for a better, more profitable life. Yes, that time felt right, but time, in the musty past, was relative.

I had a pretty good idea that this house was on the coast, in that town called Caol, Scotland. I had never heard of this town. Must be a tiny place, perhaps a fishing village? Houses in that time period had thatched roofs, and used peat moss for fuel, and oil lamps, (probably whaling oil) to light their homes. Life looked like it was hard there. People eked by, barely making it. A sense of suffocating despair constantly stole into that village like an unwelcome cold fog that slipped in under the door. That feeling of misery was an ever-present, unwanted companion, hypnotizing the struggling inhabitants into believing that hope, that powerfully precious piece of uplifting light, could not be found here.

It was cold all the time in that town. The ever-present icy-fingered wind seemed to grip the hamlet as it carried the salty air from the powerful energy of the ocean, all over the town. The steel sky weighed down any bright sunny day that would surely have been a welcome relief from those eternally leaden skies.

Rosanna

I left the address in California and suddenly I am standing in front of the same street name and number in this village of Caol, Scotland. But I am not alone.

She is such a powerful figure in that threadbare floor length, muslin nightgown; her child's body is rail thin. All I can think of when I first see her is that she must surely be chilled to the bone, but then the dead are always cold, a cold that leaves your soul tragically frozen in time and space.

I guessed her age to be about eight years old – old enough for the truth of her situation to have gripped her. Her awareness of what has happened searing her soul: the cruelest, most unjust punishment of all. Observing her from behind, I am unable to tell if she is aware that she has died, or what caused her death.

She is standing outside watching something almost as if she is gratefully removed from the moment and yet still part of it. Her back is to me. I always dread that moment when the soul turns to address me, and I can see what faced this child in her final moments. Because she is dead, the wind blowing in from the sea does not move her long black hair in any way. Her black edged nightgown does not flutter. Her stillness is unnerving, considering what is happening in front of her.

I stand beside her and ask her name. She has yet to turn to face me, only watching, emotionless, the frantic scene before her.

"My name is Rosanna."

She tells me this flatly. I automatically imagine with such a gorgeous name, that this is a beautiful child. I can see that she has porcelain skin and her gentle, black curls frame the side of her face that I can see. She turns toward me fleetingly, only long enough to acknowledge that someone is speaking to her. In that moment, I take a quick sharp breath, as if the icy Scottish air has quickly stabbed my own lungs. Part of her face is seared down to the bone. The front of her dress is burned to a sooty mess. Her hands are charred to blackness as she tried to shield herself from the inevitable aftermath of the instant hell itself was visited upon her frail body.

As I gently drape a glowing cloak about her thin shoulders, I ask her what happened. Her sweet, charming little girl voice takes me by surprise.

"I know I'm not supposed to, but I always wait up for father. I want to know that he's back from sea safe, that he's home with us again. I love him so, but he gets so angry . . . I never know, you see, I never know . . .   "This night he came home late. I fell asleep by the hearth and when I heard him open the door I ran to him, but he must have stopped by the pub. He does that sometimes and he smells of stale ale. Mother waited supper for him, but when he didn't return, she went upstairs to put the babies to bed. I could see that she was worried about him and maybe afraid, because when he comes home late and he goes to the pub he is always angry. If there is no fish, we can't eat. Mother keeps having babies. There are six of us now in this house. What will we do?"

She repeated these as facts, as children are meant to do, when they overhear their parents arguing. Rosanna, as the oldest child, would have been the one to more fully understand the family circumstances and the chronic financial problems they faced. Rosanna viewed her siblings through her parent's eyes: more mouths to feed, not blessings. The increasing pressure on her father to support his growing family must have been tremendous. Food and funds would have been difficult to come by. This would have been a very contentious house, an unhappy house. I sensed a smoldering rage just under the surface of their days.

"Rosanna, what happened that night, after he came home?"

"When I heard him open the door, I tried to hug him, to greet him, to keep him calm so he wouldn't wake the babies, but he was very drunk. He pushed me out of the way and started yelling at me. When he yelled, he woke up the babies. Mother got right up, taking care of them, but they were hungry and afraid. There wasn't much supper.

"He seemed to become even more cross as the little boys, Georgie, and Charlie, cried even louder. When baby Claire began to sob, father got even madder and he grabbed the oil lamp and threw it into the fire. The way he threw it was very strange. The oil flew out of the lamp and landed on me and father and then the lamp landed in the hearth. The fire in the hearth seemed to explode into a big, big fire. I felt like I breathed in the fire and then I was standing out here, outside, watching our house burn. Even from out here, on the street, I can hear the babies screaming.

"I can't help them.

"I think I'm dead.

"I think mother and father and all the babies are dead too.

"I think the fire killed us all.

"It seemed like a long time before someone came to help with the fire. Finally, it began to rain and then slowly, the fire went out and there was nothing left. We all died, the six of us. I don't see them, my family, but I know they died. I keep seeing the flames coming at me like a scary dragon and then I'm here. I know those scary flames came at the babies too. They're dead like me . . . they're dead like me . . ."

She repeated herself as if the reality of their deaths was something that she kept rejecting but knew she had to accept. I suspected that perhaps there was a part of her that blamed herself for all of their deaths. If only she had been able to keep him calm, but he was so unpredictable when he was drunk. This time was the worst – and the last time.

Emotionally Frozen

It doesn't matter that over 400 years had passed: this sweet child was still in shock. She was frozen in time by the stunning moment of her death. Her trauma was so great that she could not feel the emotion of the loss of her entire family. She was suspended in time by horror.

Through her eyes, I could see the flames licking the outsides of the building. The intensity of the fire was tremendous, completely engulfing the house in mere seconds. All that remained was the stone hearth. Nothing else.

I quickly found the other family members. Charles, her father, was there with his wife Dela, baby Claire, Little Charlie, and Georgie. They were all a charred mess. These souls were also in tremendous shock as well, which was why they each required extensive pre-healing before I could send them all to the Heaven World. Pre-healing enabled them to make a smoother transition and mitigated any additional emotional pain before they crossed over.

An angel cradled each of her siblings and their small bodies were healed, as Rosanna watched wordlessly. She stood as mute witness, as her sobbing parents accompanied their children to the Crossing Over point. Her father turned toward her, encouraging her to come with them. He had tears in his eyes as he extended his hand to her, but she did not make any motion toward him or the light.

"Rosanna, honey, it's time. It's time to go with your family into that wonderful light."

She looked up at me and I could see that the healing on her face and slender body was slowly beginning to restore her appearance. She never looked at the angel who gently held her once burned hands. Still frozen, she never looked back as she made her way across the Light Bridge to the Heaven World.

Now What?

What could I do now? How do I share this with the homeowner? He asked simply to be able to have a room cleared after his tenant left. He felt her energy was somewhat detrimental. The challenge was that this homeowner does not live in Scotland, had probably never been to that tiny town on the coast of Great Britain.

But he was connected. When I put the address in Google Earth, I was asked if I wanted the British or the American location. I looked at both. What were the odds? His address in California happened to be the exact same house number and street address as that tragic home in Scotland.

When I went to remote view the house in California, I was immediately taken to the house in Caol, Scotland that existed over 400 years ago. What was the connection? Dare I broach this?

No matter how I looked at this I keep coming back to the inevitable conclusion: this was not a coincidence.

Epilogue

I explained to my client that some weird supernatural linkage connected his home to a house in Scotland that burned to the ground killing six people four centuries in the past. It was pointless to speculate on what the bond was between the homes or past homeowners of both properties.

He did confirm that the dark energy he felt in his house had left and his entire home felt better. But he seemed genuinely bewildered that he could feel the energy of ghosts not only from another time, but also from an entirely different location on the Earth.

He took comfort from the fact that his seemingly innocent request for a simple clearing of his house opened the door for a towering karmic deed: releasing those six souls from their misery in the 4th dimension.

The USS Gregory

Going to the Beach

All I can see is night. I see a full moon with stars, as if I am standing on a tropical island on a warm night. I can almost feel the soft, moist air, as it would lightly cling to my skin – if I were truly standing there.

But I am there psychically to see who needs help, who cannot find their way home. I began to see them, slowly, eerily in that subtle way they appear wanting me to see them but shy at the same time.

A telltale black fog swirls around them but does not obscure the view. That black fog can mean so many things . . . a collection of souls, a tremendous evil that has befallen a location, or extreme violence that once took place here. One thing I know for sure is that the black fog is always a terrible sign.

So, I return to standing on this shore and I notice that there is an abandoned house on the beach. I also see people hiding in the bushes. Even though they are there, in an odd conundrum, I believe that they mostly have no idea that they are dead – whoever 'they' actually are. Now there are men to the right (as I face the water) who are walking up to me. There seem to be around two hundred men. Their clothes are tattered and worn. They are thin, with heavy beards but their skin is not sunburned, something you would anticipate seeing if you were on a deserted island. I get the distinct impression, that they are not used to having anyone visit them: isolation has been their norm.

They quickly leap past apprehension and embrace their curiosity. They discuss among themselves who I am and wonder if I can help them. Only one man speaks for the group. They look as if they have been left on a deserted island and have just been barely able to survive, but they are tired now.

I have a sense that I am dealing with quite a group. I begin to request Divine assistance and set up emotional sustenance: food, water, milk, bread and blankets, things that bring comfort in any dimension. The men wait for the direction of the leader. He goes toward the food as do the rest.

"Who are you, sir?" I asked.

Even from his tattered clothing, I get the sense that he is a military officer.

"They just call me Cap'n. At least I used to be their captain, their Commanding Officer. But now, without our tin can, without my command, stuck on this island, out of the action of the war – I'm not sure what I am."

"Well, Cap'n, can you tell me how you came to be on this island?" I smiled inwardly. Tin can was the universal term sailors use to describe their surface ships.

"Our ship was torpedoed by the Japanese. I remember the date: 6 September 1942. I'm pretty sure that's what happened. My command was not a large ship, not a battleship, but much smaller with a modest complement of men aboard. We had a fast frigate, you know, a small destroyer."

Perils in the Dark

"Our sonar, and our radar were manned constantly in addition to our officer of the deck watch. We were forever scanning for enemy ships, and U-boats. The seas in this part of the Pacific were dangerous. We plied them with trepidation. We were as vigilant as we could possibly be, but night is tough. We had worked hard to look out for enemy ships and subs, but by the time radar sees the sub or ship, many times it's too late. Now we know why submariners call surface ships 'targets.' We lived with the ever-constant fear that we were just sitting ducks for Jap subs.

"Guess I'm not altogether sure exactly what hit us. Was it the bombs that hit us? Or maybe it was a torpedo? Everything happened at once in the confusion of the dark. The explosions seem louder, more terrifying when you can't see the depth of the abyss that awaits you."

Physical death does not end a soul's night terror: it simply extends it. He continued his narration of their last moments as if it was only the previous night.

"When the explosions hit our ship, the stern headed into the water first and many of my men lost their lives helping others, a lot of guys who were below decks had parts of the ship fall on them and became immediately trapped inside the ship. I issued the abandon ship order and rushed my men to get off before this tin can completely sank out from under us. I was the captain and I stayed to continue to find crew members who needed help. Then, to my horror, I heard machine gun fire. I watched as the Japanese fired on my surviving men in the water, killing many of them instantly. I felt so helpless!"

"It appears that many of these men swam to this island or were adrift until they got to the island. Is that your understanding, Captain, of what happened? Did everyone get off?"

"I tried, you know? I tried my best to get everybody off, but there was no way we could survive the bombings or torpedoes that kept coming. I witnessed my men getting blown up. In the end, the moon illuminated the water enough that I saw the fish (torpedo) coming at me and I knew that momentarily I would be dead. I watched death coming at me and there was no place to go, no escape, no rescue. No miracle was ever going to save us.

"I remember the flash of the explosion and then all of a sudden, I was on this island, which is probably Guadalcanal based on our last fix. But I'm not sure. Are islands the same in life and death? Is this island real just for my men? I mean, I know I'm dead, but these guys, these brave dumb guys, my loyal crew, they think they got off that tin can alive and that they're just waitin' on this island for a ship to come and rescue us – but no ship is ever coming for you when you're dead. I haven't had the heart to tell them that none of us made it. Is that cowardly of me? I guess I'm afraid if they know that they died that they would give up all hope and then – well I've got no idea what happens when you're already dead and give up hope. I don't know how any of this works. Is that why you're here? Are you going to rescue us?"

"Perhaps rescue is as good a word as any and, in the case of your men, it's the easiest way to help them to cross over and accept the help that is coming."

"God, I hope so. These guys comb the beaches, climb the mountains on this island, ever the diligent lookouts, thinking that we've only been here for a couple of days and that the Navy is going to send a rescue craft. But I know that nothing's ever coming for us. I never had the heart to tell them that this island is their hell and their eternity. Hope is all they have. At least they still follow my lead . . . even in death.

"When I saw you on the beach, I thought that maybe you could help us. I mean, geez, you're all bright and glowy . . . Obviously you don't belong here, and you didn't show up in any ship or plane, so you must be from some heavenly place. Nothing here glows. Every moment feels like the last."

The Burden of Command

The pathway to crossing over is always facilitated with the comfort of the things that are laid out. The buffet of sorts was filled with all kinds of wonderful comfort food. This brought all the men together in addition to the request from their Captain to assemble.

As the sailors came forward and started to eat, an angel who served them not only food, but also clean clothing and a warm jacket greeted each of them. Even on a tropical island in the Pacific, there is a solid coldness to death. These mariners, who honestly believed they survived the ship blast, were stunned in that electric moment of coming face to face with a seven-foot angel. They suddenly realized that they died; that they wouldn't be going home to friends and families, girlfriends, or the family dog, that life on earth for them was over.

The savage wounds that torpedoes and bombs inflict on a person's body were gradually healed. The catastrophic injuries disappeared, and the elegance of the human body was restored.

Each sailor readily walked wide-eyed with his angel across the Light Bridge to the Heaven World.

"Well, Captain, are you ready?"

"Yes, I'm ready, too. And thank you. I guess my prayers were answered because you're here. I've always felt guilty that I couldn't save my men, couldn't get them rescued from whatever island we landed on, but now, at least I guess we're rescued. I'm just curious: how long have we been here, wherever 'here' is?"

"72 years. Blessedly, you didn't feel that passage of time."

"Thank God our prayers were answered. Thank you again. I'm ready."

We Are the Same in Life and in Death

We are the same in death as in life. Military people will continue to seek approval and follow their chain of command. Officers will continue to lead their men because that sense of eternal responsibility for your men, your crew, never leaves you. This captain continued to shoulder the emotional burden of command, maintaining hope for his men, even in death.

This entire experience was the result of a client who had a bad, nagging feeling, a sense that there was someone with him and insisted that I look at his home and him personally. He was convinced that there was more than one person there and that there was some type of violence attached to whatever I would find. While he was connected to the Navy, he had no idea why this entire ghostly scenario was attached to him. Sometimes you aren't going to know why a ghost attaches to you. It simply happens. If nothing else, it provides an opportunity to be of service to souls whom you have never met, would never have met, and would never know – and yet . . . and yet, you are called upon to help them, positively changing the course of their eternity.

Epilogue

The USS Gregory

I looked up information about ships that sank on that date in the Pacific. I may have found it, but it is hard to know for sure. Some information is different. It looks like it may have been the USS Gregory, which was sunk by the Japanese on Sept. 5, 1942. The stern sunk first, Japanese ships fired upon her, but no subs fired upon her, but how could we really know that? Japanese aircraft shot at the men in the water as they left their sinking ships. There was no time for lifeboats. Many men may have survived by swimming to the island of Guadalcanal. Perhaps many died there as well. And now it is over.

An Acre of Haunted Ground

Nothing Grows!

"We're desperate! This house is a damn nightmare! We need you to do something about this. Don't tell me 'this is all just coincidence.' There has to be a logical explanation for the utterly unexplainable!

"We're chronically tired, and we fight constantly. It feels like we're all going nuts. No one sleeps at night; our kids have nightmares night after night. Jeff and I feel as if there is something unexplainable that bothers us as we sleep. We wake up irritable and exhausted.

"This is a brand-new house, for God's sake! Yet, we have one water problem after the other: our sinks leak, and we had to replace our brand-new hot water heater. Our finances are in ruins, bills keep coming in, and there's no money.

"I feel as if the ground is cursed, no - I'm convinced of it. I love gardening but nothing grows! We're even afraid of some of the trees in the yard. Other trees on this acre of ground are struggling to survive. The twin oaks that should be 'gracing' our property are actually threatening our property to the extent that we're afraid to walk near them. My husband is fearful that the rotted top parts of those trees are going to fall down on us.

"Oh, and I feel like someone is watching me all the time, like he's deliberately haunting me, day, and night. It's the creepiest feeling. I'm going nuts. That's it: I'm going nuts! I feel like Jeff and I bought the house from hell!"

My client, Kelly blurts out all of this so quickly, I couldn't stop her. She raced to the end of her sentences, as if she was competing with herself to get all the details out before someone or something stopped her, or she lost her nerve. She desperately wanted to tell someone who would not believe she was crazy, who would not direct her back to conventional logic and accepted science. Sometimes there is no logical explanation for supernatural phenomena.

"Are your children reacting to these things or is it just you and your husband? Do your children and your husband see or sense someone watching them, too?"

"Yes, but they didn't want to tell me at first. I feel angry all the time and I think they didn't want to upset me with one more thing."

Listening to Kelly's emotions explode in a pent-up torrent of rage and fear, it's becoming apparent that this small plot of ground in the deep south is taking its toll on the living and the dead.

"Alright Kelly, you know I do believe you and, of course, I'll be glad to take a look and get back to you. Just checking though, is your husband on board with this remote view?"

"Right now, I wouldn't care if he agrees or not, but yes, thank God he does agree. When the third faucet broke, he said that was it, we had to figure it out. The plumber said there was no reason for any of these things to break or fail. None. That did it, so yes, you have his support as well. Help us, please help us."

Holding the Energy of the Past

Huntersville is a small town not far from Charlotte in the Piedmont region of North Carolina. This growing town of generously wide streets, beautiful, stately trees, and old homes with welcoming front porches, looks deceptively peaceful. It is a growing town, with developers opening up new subdivisions here and there. Kelly's acre property is in one of these new developments. I should have been able to see her freshly built house immediately. But that was not what I saw.

The energy of different events on this land was so compelling that several stacks of time seemed to swirl in front of me. I was eventually able to work backwards to the oldest imposing energy.

Finally, the originating energy seemed to come from a stack of time reflecting the brutal aftermath of the Civil War.

Roughly 1869: The Slave Ghosts' Stories

"We been waitin' a long time. I's Buck, that's what they call me, Buck. I reckon they's about 35 of us standing 'round just waitin'. Light Lady, we's so glad you come. We believe that you'll hep' us ta' leave here. We hate it here. It's dark, scary an' lonely. We don't knows why so many people been hate'n us these years. Why some people wanna hurt us? Why was we killed in that horrible way? We all died in different ways but all them people who kilt us, hated us. We don't find no peace in life and we ain't findin' no peace in death. Maybe you can hep us ta' find peace."

"Who are you all?"

"We's slaves. Our graves be in this here corner of the property. We be right pleased to be able ta' tell ya our story. When you's a slave, nobody much cares what happens to ya'. Once they kilt us, they buried us real fast, right here. We can't seem ta' leave here. We be seein' dark things 'round us all the time. We be scared, ma'am real scared.

"We wants to tell ya how we come to be here. We be thankin' ya fer bein' kind ta us, something we all find real strange. How come you's so bright, you glows? You some kinda angel?"

"No, I'm not an angel, just someone glad to be of service to you all. Tell me, how did you all die?"

Buck looked around at the others.

"I guess it's kinda up ta' me ta' explain it. I tells ya, ma'am. Somehow, we done lived through the Civil War. We hoped that things'd be better when it be done, but after President Lincoln done died, all them white folks started haten' us even more. They blamed us for lossin' their plantations and farms. There t'weren't no food for white or Negro. Them Union soldiers burned our slave quarters, so t'weren't no place ta' go, no place to live. I reckon them Yankees thought they was helpin' us burning our slave shack but after that burnin' we ain't got no place to sleep, no land, no food, no clothes.

"People thought we was stealin' their food. We begged for food, but no one would give us no food. We was starvin' to death. We did take food sometimes. We did. We was all just so hungry. May, over here was whipped so bad that we reckon she died from infection from her wounds. Big John – they hanged him. He don't know why. They shot me 'cause I was stealin' a chicken. Them over yonder – they all died when the shack they was hidin' in burned plum ta' the ground. We all gots our stories. Ya' gots to understand, these was hard times, hard times.

"This here land was part of a big plantation that grew 'bacca an' cotton, fruits an' vegetables. When we was livin' on the plantation, there was always plenty of food. Oh, and we had our own gardens too and we could grow food we liked. We worked hard, we did, but we had food ta' eat and some place to sleep. It was bad. But after the war, we was cast out. Crazy people be roamin' the country and them rebels shot some of us on sight. Some of our families fled on the Underground Railroad up North, but we figured we could maybe make it here after the war, maybe start new. But we just died, all of us that you see here."

"I have come to help a couple who seem to be living in a haunted house. Can you all see a house?"

"No, ma'am, we don't see no house. When we was livin' and dyin' here, naw, it t'weren't here. We can't see it, musta' been built after we died. No one cared about markin' the grave of a slave, so no one knowed after a few years that we was even buried here. I reckon we was lucky to even get buried."

"Buck, were there a pair of twin oak trees here on this property?"

"Yeah, we can see 'em too, over yonder, but they be right small trees. The trees that we mostly se'ed, be the big oak trees where we was hung over yonder."

"Thank you, Buck. Now, I'm here to help you all find your way home out of this darkness. Are you ready to finally go home to the Heaven world?"

Buck and the others looked to see a growing light that seemed to be moving toward them. Angels draped blankets over their weary shoulders.

"Yes, ma'am we is. Is that what it looks like? That light over yonder? It's kinda like you opens a door fo us.

"I can see my Ma standing there. May can ya' see your Pa? Hey Big John, is that your boy waitin' for ya? Lordy, Lordy, there be my grammy! I ain't never – never 'xpected ta' see my whole family!"

Before Buck took those final steps into the light, he turned to me.

"Thank ya' kindly for this here blanket. We all be real grateful to feel warm. Thank ya' Light Lady. Maybe someday you'all get ta' know what this meant ta' us, what it means ta' finally get ta' go home."

Tears began to weave their way down his cheeks as he walked faster and faster and then began to run toward his mother and grandmother and other family members who gathered to greet him. All of them behaved as if shackles had been removed from their very souls and their happiness set them free.

Slaves endured tremendous privation, humiliation, and depression. The Civil War set them free politically but did not allow them to feel that they were totally liberated men and women: they could not vote or have the benefit of the judicial system to resolve conflict. The days of Reconstruction after the war saw horrific things happen to entire families. The violence of their deaths kept them bound in darkness in the 4th dimension. Crossing over freed them in every sense of the word.

Burying murdered men and women on this ground spiritually and energetically poisoned this land for anyone who would try to live or farm on this acreage. Now I understood. No wonder nothing grew. Sometimes I wonder if the Earth itself stays in mourning when the murdered are placed in shallow graves, and when the blood of the dead seeps into the ground.

Fifty Years Later, around 1919

It was around 1919 (before it became Huntersville), and this same piece of property in Mecklenburg County, North Carolina, was sold to a young white couple as farmland. (Negroes, blacks, non-whites whatever term you use, were seldom allowed to borrow money to own their own land even fifty years later.) The previous scene slips away and I find myself watching a young woman walking around the wide front porch of a dirty looking, two story house.

She's a thin woman with dull looking, dark brown hair that hangs limply on her boney shoulders. Her filthy white cotton dress comes to her ankles. I guessed her age to be around 30 years old. I noticed that the dirty energy of severe depression hung about her as I asked her to tell me her story. Her name was Bobby June.

"Carl and I hadn't been married too long and since we grew up near here, we decided to settle here, you know, near our families. We was real lucky to be able to purchase this bit of land. We wanted to farm it; it's a right pretty area. There used to be a plantation near here, a while back growin' cotton and tobacca'. We was so hopeful we could grow that too. . . but as we tried to farm, absolutely nothing would grow exceptin' the most-stubborn weeds. I had a kitchen garden with 'taters, onions, 'maters, squash, but it all died, all of it."

She looked away with resignation, as if she could see her dreams for the future evaporating with the morning dew. Her soft southern drawl was edged with regret.

"We done built a house, a little two-story clapboard. Our friends helped us put it up. I had a right nice kitchen and an icebox. We even had a parlor. We had faith that the land would be good to us so maybe we could expand the house when children came.

"But we produced empty fields not children. Carl got more and more depressed. We felt like the land was cursed. There weren't never 'nough rain. Our seed wouldn't grow. The oak trees, those pretty twin oaks down yonder as you come up to the house are growing, but even they struggled.

"Carl started drinkin' and his rages got worse and worse. Then he started beatin' me. I wanted to leave here, but there weren't no money: we couldn't even pay for our seed no more. I wanted to leave him, but there weren't no place to go. My family was too poor to take me back.

"We done sold all we could to try an hold on. We even tried sellin' the house, but no one wanted it. One night my husband told me that the voices he was hearin' in his head wouldn't stop. I figured that the house was haunted, and I just wanted to walk away from it all. But his pride wouldn't let him. He didn't want to leave our home and feel like a failure. When I tried to talk to him when he weren't drunk, he'd scream at me and come after me. I didn't know him anymore: he wasn't the sweet Carl I married.

"Finally, he beat me so often, that one night, he plum beat me to death. I don't know if beaten' me helped him to feel better, but he was a different person when the drink took him over.

"Once I died, I saw all of these terrible dark things everywhere. I was so scared. I realized I could see my husband and those vicious things that were tormentin' him, makin' him do bad things. I didn't know how to help him.

"I don't rightly know how long I had been dead before the tax collector showed up demandin' that Carl pay the taxes on the land. Carl knew there weren't no money for taxes. That night, Carl drank so much, and he was so angry, that he just got his huntin' rifle out and he killed hisself. Once he joined me here in this awful dark place, he was so sorry for what he had done. I reckon he felt a terrible guilt. But his bein' sorry don't much help us. We been stuck here ever since. We're here, walkin' around the house, where we died. Stuck. It was a long time 'afore anyone come to find our bodies. They buried us in a corner of the property. They weren't no money for a real Christian burial.

"Light Lady, I got to tell ya' that it feels good to get tell somebody what happened to us. We're real grateful now that we ain't got to stay here no longer. Once you come to find us, them dark creatures done left us alone. There be light ahead. Maybe I'll get to see my family. Finally, we can go home."

She concluded her story almost flatly as if she was so emotionally numb that she had to find that place in her heart to remind her that she was loved and there would be family to welcome her home, to embrace her.

When murder and suicide are committed on any piece of property these actions inevitably open a portal to the lower astral, the realms of the hells. Through that door come all kinds of creatures called Lower Realm Intelligences, and there can be hundreds of them. These beings feed on the energy of soul misery. Three feet high, they resemble sooty black monsters with red eyes. They torment the dead by constantly coming at them in a threatening manner with claw like hands.

These horrifying creatures make their presence known to living people in the sleep state, causing them to never have a whole night's sleep. During the day, they linger just outside the realm of vision. The person thinks they see something but can't be sure. The sooty black energy they bring, clogs mechanical things, causing endless problems. When they are around, the homeowner will have problems with faucets, toilets, and any type of water pump.

These beings feed on the energy of acts of violence. It is the endless buffet of cruelty that keeps them going and they use that energy to create a nightmare for the living no matter when that might be.

Only clearing the earth and assisting the tragically dead to cross over deprives these Lower Realm beings of food and forces them to leave. This is why living people feel so much better after someone helps tortured souls to cross over.

The Modern Protector

There could have been other things that happened on that property before the slaves were murdered and buried there but I did not see anything else. Bobbie June and Carl's house simply fell into ruin. The land was toxic physically and spiritually because people in different time frames were murdered or committed suicide and were buried there. The land was never cleared.

Now that all of those souls and those Lower Realms were removed, I scanned the property again to see if there was anything or anyone else still there. The saga continued.

The decades passed, and a developer bought this and other huge tracts of land and began to build homes on this area around 2005. It is ironic that no one actually lived on that land between 1919 and 2005. The first new house was built on the acre of land that included the slave burial ground, and the house where the couple died and were buried.

My clients, who moved into this new house on this same piece of property, did not realize that they also brought a ghost with them: the wife's grandfather who, upon his death, did not move into the light. He remained with his granddaughter to 'help' her.

"I'm so glad you're here! I'm Tom, maybe you can help me to help my granddaughter and her family. I've been worried about them for so long. I've known that I should move into the light when it comes for me and it comes for me often, but I don't feel anyone in this family is safe. I was going to stick around for a little while and look out for her. I know that she saw me in the mirror now and then, but no matter, I'm here for her."

"Why are you worried about them? Why do you feel they aren't safe?"

"Well, it's the strangest thing. I – I don't exactly know how to describe it, or them. These little dark beings about three feet high with skinny arms and long claws come at my daughter and her family. They're scary and I can seem them, but the grandkids, Kelly and Jeff only seem to sense an evil around them. I watch these 'creatures' come out at night and dance around their beds while they're sleeping. That's when I go into action, shooing them – the dark guys – away. Sometimes I work all night! During the day, the dark guys mess with the water pipes and appliances, anything mechanical. It looks to me like they spray this black film on things and then, after that, there are problems.

"I can't figure out why the kids bought property that's so bad. Sometimes these dark guys come at me too and I fight them off. I try to help, I really do, but nothing I do seems much help. Do you know how to get rid of these dark beings?"

"Yes sir, I do know how to remove them. See? They're gone now. Other people were murdered on this property and that energy of murder – oh and there was a suicide as well – opened up a doorway to a dark place. That's where these inky creatures, these Lower Realm Intelligences come from. But they've been removed. The land is healing now, and your daughter and her family can begin to rebuild their life without all this darkness."

"I can't tell you how relieved I am that Jeff and Kelly and the kids will be alright, that they'll be safe, and that it's okay for me to move on. I can join my other family members waiting for me. It's such a relief to just let go. Thanks for your help."

Epilogue

Toxic predecessor energy accumulates on land that has been the site of repeated tragedies, and this property carried the energy of many violent deaths. It takes four to five hundred years for the Earth to begin to clear the land of the trauma that it experienced, without specific spiritual intervention.

Graves also stress the land, holding the decomposing bodies for an endless period of time. The negativity of a graveyard has been visited on many a homeowner who ends up buying land that has be 'reclaimed' from a cemetery. Given a choice, few people would ever want to own a home built a home on cemetery land.

Murder stressed the land because of the energy of severe violence.

War traumatizes an entire area.

Even families that scream at and hate each other distress the home and land in which they live. Healing any property also helps all the adjacent minerals, the soil, the plants, and the animals in the area to recover. Part of restoration includes transitioning the dead from every stack of time and removing the Lower Realm Intelligences.

Trees nestle their roots in the earth, feel how the soil breathes and do not get a choice where the squirrel or a homeowner plants their acorns. The tree has to 'make do' with the energy that surrounds it. Even though people do seem to choose where to 'plant' themselves, they are also often surprised when they are 'stuck' with a toxic house, both spiritually and emotionally.

The healthier and more positive the earth, the more vibrant are the trees, and the twin oaks began to recover. The old dead parts of both trees were removed by a tree expert the family hired, which seemed to lift a great burden from this stalwart pair of silent witnesses. New branches formed, and the trees soon became robust and healthy as they proudly framed the entrance to this now beautiful looking property. Jeff and Kelly's yard was also now more vibrant, and things were beginning to come into bloom for their yard and their lives.

Finances improved; water problems ceased. A wonderful night's sleep became the family norm instead of the exception and they all stopped fighting with each other. They noticed that they no longer felt as if someone was watching them.

This young family was now free of that terrible haunting feeling that an unresolved sadness was surrounding them. By making the request for help, this couple did a tremendous service to all of those souls and a great service to the land.

The House in Pasadena

"Hi Tina, just checking in and letting you know that we bought this charming little house that sits perched on a modest hill on a quiet street in Old Pasadena. I love the energy here; it feels so peaceful. It has those old narrow hardwood floors. The doorways to each room are arched in that charming 1920s architecture. It has an adorable kitchen with original tile and although it's not an 'open concept' it still feels warm and inviting and so comfortable. The outside landscaping needs some work but overall, the plants seem healthy, there are flowers everywhere and a cozy sense to the whole place. We feel so happy here.

"I wish you could actually come here and see it. I'm having it Feng Shuied, but I thought that I would also get you to remote view it to make sure that there isn't someone here from the past."

"It doesn't sound like you're feeling anything negative. Are you seeing or sensing anything?" Normally, I don't even ask these few questions, but I wanted to hear her on another level.

"Nope, not a thing, but I do want you to look just to be sure, as part of good Feng Shui. Even before I have my Feng Shui consultant come out, I want to make sure that the spaces are absolutely clear."

"Glad to help. I'll let you know what I find."

Such Good Energy

This client is always so conscientious about helping the dead. She has lived in several places and she always has me clear her homes. Her psychic ability is growing, and this increasing sensitivity seems to be making her far more receptive to sensing the presence of a ghost. However, in this case, she had not consciously felt anything. The energy of the house seemed wonderful. She genuinely loved this place. Maybe, just maybe there was nothing there. That would be amazing.

Psychically standing in front of this home, I got the feeling of a charming bungalow although it was a bit large to be considered a bungalow. While the rooms were small, they seemed well appointed and well cared for over the multiple decades. The neighborhood was kept up, with gorgeous, elegantly appointed homes and yards. This location had held its property values over time with a wonderful look and feel.

I slipped into the time stream of this pretty place and immediately felt how wonderful the energy was here. There was no violence, no anger, no pain, and no heartache. I took a deep, relaxing breath. I reminded myself that the entire Pasadena area has never been home to wars, violence, riots, or mass tragedies. Its claim to fame is the Tournament of Roses Parade. Once a year thousands of excited people full of hope gather to inhale the creativity of nature adorning stunning, creatively designed, aromatic, parade floats as they wind their way through a city that time has beautifully respected over the years. The United States starts every New Year in this pretty city, this lovely town of flowery expectation for the days ahead.

While I found myself completely open to whatever might be here, I was also aware that there just might not be anything here at all, and although that has never happened in all the houses, I have remote viewed, there is always a first time. Perhaps . . .

"Tea, anyone?"

She would have been elderly in 1920. Her era most likely was Victorian, based on her clothing. She wore her special occasion outfit: an elegantly appointed black taffeta floor-length skirt with a beautiful rose-colored wide satin ribbon around her tiny waist. She would have made a rustling sound as she walked, her skirt so formally done. Her stunning cream shirt was sewn with all types of intricate lace and pearl buttons down the front of a high collar. The exceptionally large gold-rimmed cameo she wore at her neck was typical of the style in that age, that age of proper civility, exceptional hospitality, and the luxury of unhurried time stretching before you in patient days. The only give away was a tiny bit of something red on her shirt, almost as if she had sneezed with a bloody nose.

Her welcoming face was rimmed in soft wisps of grey curls. The rest of her long hair was neatly piled in a proper bun on top of her head. She was tiny, truly a wisp of a woman. Her bony hands automatically grabbed the sterling silver tea pot and began filling an elegant, bone china teacup as she asked me to come in and sit awhile in her parlor and tell her why I was there.

This stream of time brought me back roughly to the turn of the last century. As I watched her hand me a starched white linen napkin to lie on my lap, I realized that this lovely lady had been serving tea in this parlor, today's living room, for 90 years of mortal time. But time stood still for her.

The tea was always hot, brewed, and ready to serve.

Her teatime biscuits and cakes did not look old but freshly baked and filled with buttery goodness, homemade jam, and powdered sugar. I was sure they smelled delicious.

But alas, I was not there for a long conversation, tea, or cakes. I was there to help her cross over.

"Thank you so much for the tea, and what is your name?"

"Cora. It was my Grandmother's name on my father's side, God rest her soul. What brings you here, dear? I love having visitors, especially on Sunday afternoons. I always serve tea and my butter-jam cakes. Have one, they're delicious!"

"Thank you, Cora, but I'm not here for tea. I'm here . . ." I felt my voice trail away. I felt suddenly constrained, stopped. How do I tell her that I'm here to inform her that she is dead . . . that very possibly, that bit of red on her shirt was either blood she coughed up or sneezed out, that killed her as she sat there. It was the telltale sign of death by consumption, as it would have been called in her time, or tuberculosis. Sometimes a person simply fell into a coma and died, their lungs giving way. She obviously had no idea she was dead.

Time to try again: I came up with a better idea, a more appropriate one for a very proper lady.

"I brought a guest with me. Let me introduce you. Cora, meet Bright Angel. She's brought you a gift, a beautiful shawl for your shoulders."

"An angel . . . then . . ."

Yes, I thought to myself, the angel means you're dead and in that astonishing moment of reality you begin to approach acceptance, or finality and ultimately embrace the comfort of death in a kindly way. It seems that she accepted her death right away, but in her realm, there is no time as we think of it. The time it took her to appreciate the new dynamic of her situation is not relevant in this timeless dimension.

"Yes, I have brought you a companion to help you cross that beautiful light bridge you see just there. Perhaps as you cross that bridge you will get to see your family, your grandmother. How does that sound?"

She looked up at the angel and accepted the warm gift gently placed around her. She then allowed herself to be guided over the light bridge to the Heaven World. All thoughts of tea and cakes, visitors and quiet days were gone in that glorious blaze of light and peace.

Red Hawk

All right, one ghost in the living room. Let me see who else has taken refuge in this pretty cottage, I thought to myself, as I continued to explore each room of this home. Reaching the master bedroom, scanning the entire perimeter of the space, I was pretty astonished to see the next other dimensional visitor. I also could not help but wonder why my friend was unable to sense this person.

"Excuse me, can you see me?" I asked this newest ghost.

"Yes."

Okay, obviously a man of few words, but then based on what he was wearing he probably was not a chatty person in life, either.

"How did you come to be in this house? What did your tribe call you?" I found him standing, bewildered, in the master bedroom. He wore buckskin clothing, a knife at his belt and moccasins. I had no idea how long he had been standing there - waiting for something to happen.

"Chief called me Red Hawk. I have eyes like hawk. I watched wagon train, and people who come into Arapaho lands. I was with my Chief and men of tribe. We attacked the soldiers guarding a wagon train. Chief said we had to keep white people from taking our lands and killing buffalo. When fight was over, I kept watching the people; I followed the wagon train to here. I keep watching these white people."

"Do you realize, Red Hawk, that you died in the fight with the Army and the wagon train?"

"Yes, soldier bullet hit my body. I saw it lying on the ground, my body. It felt strange to see my strong body lying there. How can one tiny hole in chest kill a strong man?"

"I know. Even tiny ones can be very deadly. What do you see as you look around where you are standing? Who are you watching right now?"

"I see settlers in the distance camping. This is high bluff, and they cannot see me. I keep watching them. But I cannot find my Chief. I do not know if he died. No one comes for me. I am not sure what I am supposed to do next. Can you help me? The settlers are not doing anything else. They keep making the camp and nothing changes. I am tired, very tired. Will you help me?"

As I watched him cross over, I marveled that my client never felt or sensed the presence of either of these two ghosts. I was now curious about what else I would find in this seemingly unassuming little house.

The Epidemic

I began to explore the other two bedrooms in this modest home and immediately found a seven-year-old girl. She was wearing a long white nightgown and seemed to be profoundly sad.

"Can you help me find my mommy? I keep looking for her, but I can't find her. I saw her not long ago and now it's dark and I'm afraid. Where did she go?"

"I'll be happy to help you find your mom. Come with me. Let's see if she's just in the next room. Oh, what's your name?"

"Mabel."

We found her mom in the other bedroom, still in a bed, looking ill and in pain. I never knew her name, only that she could not see her daughter.

I felt strongly that they both of died of influenza in what must have been the pandemic of 1918. They were both wearing long white nightgowns, looked extremely pale, gaunt, and miserable. Neither fully grasped that death had taken them to the 4th dimension and that time no longer existed. Neither mother nor daughter left the rooms they died in, despite the fact that each thought they were searching for the other. Once these ghosts were reunited, neither had any problem seeing the other.

"Here we are Mabel, here's your mom. Looks like she's been ill too. Would you like to climb in bed with her and be with her for a few minutes while I bring in someone to help you both feel better?"

"Yes! Mommy? I missed you so much. I've been looking and looking for you in the darkness. Where were you Mommy? Why did you leave me?"

It was so gratifying to see Mabel seem to snuggle next to her dead mother but in the environs of the 4th dimension, death doesn't seem real. Death is a word that has no meaning for a child who only needs the loving comfort of her mother. And her mother was equally delighted to see her adorable daughter.

"Oh sweetie, I was so sick, I didn't mean to leave you, to let you be by yourself, but I was so ill, I . . . I think I didn't make it and I think you didn't make it either."

"Sure, we did, Mommy, we're here together. It's all okay now, Mommy, but it's still dark except for that light over there. Can you walk, Mommy, so we can go find that light?"

As they happily made their way to the healing light of God, the mom turned to me and said thank you and then they were gone.

Epilogue

Obviously little Mabel and her mom were unable to see Cora or the Native American. Mabel and her mother could not even see each other, and they died in the same house in the same period of time, but then this is not unusual. Each thought they were totally alone.

Loneliness and confusion come when a soul has no understanding of what to do in death. This is one of the most tragic things that any psychic can see. Helping them to find the light, to leave a mortal location and become free of the constraints of the 4th dimension shifts the energy in any area.

My friend's house was now completely clear. If it felt wonderful before, it would surely feel fantastic now.

When I shared with my client the stories I gleaned from her four ghosts, she was astonished.

"I had no idea we had any ghosts here much less four! How could they possibly be here in all of those different times, and me not feel a thing? How is that possible?"

"There is one potential explanation: each was stuck in a peaceful stack of time and that energy had a minimal impact on the current time. Believe me, this was not what I would have expected."

And so, the house in Pasadena will go on being charming, warm, and welcoming, but without its ghostly residents. Blessedly, they are now safe, secure, and healed, in the Heaven World, especially Cora. Cora may have died serving tea. Her transition was so elegantly simple that I smile to myself. How I wish all the souls I transition could experience such a simple crossing. How wonderful to not have a horribly traumatized body or horrific pain and suffering.

Silent Sentinel

No two requests to remove ghosts are ever the same. When the call comes in, it is always the routine plea for help, the plea to not think the requester is 'weird,' 'crazy' or 'paranoid,' and of course, the desire to know how quickly the 'clearing' can be done. Straightforward – right? The person simply wants the situation rectified so that the person and/or their family can return to normal.

But the world of the paranormal is precisely that: 'para' normal, meaning that it is beyond what anyone would consider 'normal,' even in the most general sense. People come to me because what they are feeling and experiencing is way outside that supposedly 'routine' paradigm. My job is to return their property and (hopefully) their lives to some level of what is considered an acceptable 'norm.'

Clients are often so frustrated with a

paranormal situation because no one else believes them, or what they are struggling with, that they blurt out all of the clues. It is human nature for them to want to share what frightens them. But that desire to share instantly creates an ethics issue for me: How does the homeowner know if what I am seeing (or any psychic for that matter,) is because of what they shared at the beginning of the conversation or because I really saw something in the ether and removed it?

The best plan is to preclude the ethics issue completely. Therefore, I have a very strict policy: I don't to ask any questions because I don't want the homeowner to reveal any information. I also ask the homeowners not to volunteer any details. I walk a very fine line here. Usually, all I request is an address and whether or not both spouses and/or partners have given permission for me to perform this service. It is important that both homeowners agree to this process so that everyone knows that I will 'be there,' in their home on an etheric level. If someone is renting a home, I need permission of both renters but not necessarily the property owner. If someone is paying for living in a dwelling, in any way, then he and/or she has the right to live there in psychic peace.

Yet, sometimes in conversation, there is a seemingly casual clue, a hint of something more, of something critically important. And in this case, the homeowner, Sandy, mentioned that she has suffered from chronic migraines for what seemed like forever. She off-handedly wondered if clearing the ghosts could possibly help with her headaches. I responded that I had no idea whether or not there could be a connection. Sandy and her husband asked that I scan the entire property and examine what, if anything was going on there that could be influencing them today.

This couple lived on 10 acres of property in Suffolk, Virginia, property that had been in her family for more than 150 years. This fact instantly alerted me to the possibility of there being ghosts from either the Revolutionary War and/or the Civil War. Any area that has been an unwilling host to such important historical conflict will carry the resonance of violence. How that will affect individual homeowners is unique to each situation.

Believe it or not, there are actually places on the Earth that are not haunted, that are not filled with darkness or have been Native American burial grounds, battlefields, church graveyards or had a violent act take place on them. There are psychically clean, lovely places to live. Yes, of course those places exist . . . but it could not be found on this tragic piece of property. No, I already had a strong sense that I would not be finding peace on this acreage in the Heart of Dixie.

150 Years of Unchanging Ground

As I began my remote view, I carefully looked around to get a feel for the entire piece of property as well as the surrounding area. I can see two houses on this land, one is a rental and the other is the client's home. I know these two houses are only there in current-day time. I can feel the presence of this reality. It is a strange thing this ability to discern what is real in which stack of time. Both houses are real only in this current stack of time. And I know this because both houses melt into the future as I ask to be shown the influencing stack of time exerting the most power on this piece of property. These houses truly do not exist in the past.

My scan of the countryside revealed towering oak, sycamore, hickory, and pine trees: a lush and bountiful looking landscape. This heavily wooded land changed very little until the advent of the Civil War, that pesky historical blotch of darkness that is sabotaging this tragic 1860s era stack of time. Patiently I watch as a new scene unfolds. I am now beginning to understand what is influencing my client. Upon closer inspection, I can see the cotton fields that surround the entire area and I know with a sickening sense that this is slave country.

Perhaps that was the catalyst: slavery itself. Slavery, the darkness that was that societal norm of the South, from the time of the early settlement of the Americas, was casting an echoing sadness on the land. Maybe that was the attracting energy, the magnet for death and misery that makes this particular 10 acres a sorrowful place to live.

As I approached the property line, I could see them, acres, and acres of them.

The Watchers Are Here

Scanning the scene under a starry night canopy, I realize that this is what it looked like in roughly 1862: acres of campfires as far as the eye can see with thousands of men camped here. It feels to be the middle of the night; there are only men on watch. I recognize the smell of hickory wood burning and hear the faint crackling as the logs turn to embers and the embers crumble as the fires ebb away. The faint aroma of chicory coffee mingles with the unmistakable whiff of horses tied up in the distance. Even horses become battle weary after so much war. The loud snores of soldiers in desperate need of rest punctuate the night as they sleep in tents lined up in neat, disciplined military rows. This brief sleep is their only relief from the daily fear that tomorrow could bring their inevitable death. This Confederate campground is a welcome respite before tomorrow's upcoming battle, wherever that will be. But these men are blissfully unaware that they are not alone in their sleep.

The watchers are here. They drift silently from tent to tent, keeping a watchful eye as these mortal men sleep. The watchers think they are not sleepy, do not need rest. Some gather around the campfire and stare at the smoldering ruins of the moment, never realizing that for them, this moment is all that is left.

Briefly reliving the intensity of that last fatal day, each wispy soldier wonders what tomorrow will bring; remaining unaware that tomorrow will never come. Each one is oblivious to their fatal condition, dead men hoping for the miracle of surviving the battle, that miracle of continued life that can never come. Some are staying with buddies, friends, and family members to protect them as they did in life. Some simply returned to the encampment when the previous battle reached its ignominious end, gruesomely unaware of their fate. Other soldiers, frozen in the moment of death, are still battling on in some bankrupt farmer's blood-soaked field near this encampment. Some know they're dead; some will never figure it out.

Perhaps the men who die in tomorrow's battle of butchery will return to the campfires in the evening thinking they are also still alive. But they're all dead now, both those living during that archaic era, as well as those who died before I got to that campground.

Standing Watch

Angels afforded all of the dead soldiers the peace of final release from the initial moment of their passing. The removal of all of the ghosts in the fields surrounding the two houses will help the land to be much clearer without the burden of the chronic energy of death.

Returning to the present, I quickly assisted any lingering Civil War soldiers who were in the red brick rental house, left over from that previous stack of time. Ghosts from the past can and do influence current owners of any property. How can a soldier from 1862 be in a current-day house at the same time as 21st century homeowners? They can do this, because ghosts of the past and mortal people living in the present can occupy the same space because they are separated by time and are not necessarily aware of each other's presence. The only thing that current-day people may notice is that there is some type of energy shift, which can take the form of feeling, sensing, seeing, or smelling something. A homeowner can also see something or someone out of the corner of his or her eye.

Arriving at the owner's older white-sided, green-roofed house on a different part of the property, I scanned it for ghosts. Entering the front door, I scanned the first floor, including the old fashioned screened in porch: so far, no ghosts. Toward the back of the house were stairs going up to the second floor.

I scanned every room on this floor and began to believe that by clearing this Southern encampment of all of the Confederates, I had already cleared this home. But despite the thousands who had in fact already been escorted to the Heaven World, there was one poor soul I had not previously seen, and I instantly realized why I missed him. I needed to see him, to see where he was and with whom. Meaning that had I simply moved him on with the other large group, I might never have appreciated how critical it was to see him above all of the other ghosts on this property. He was important and I believe I was guided to find him to help this homeowner.

He looked to be roughly 18 years old, a Private in Jeff Davis' Confederate Army. His uniform was intact but still held the muddy patches of dirt from the last battle. Standing watch, his rifle was close by his side, and his head was bowed forward. From the front, he looked as if he had simply fallen asleep on watch. (Surely his First Sergeant would have his hide.) But upon closer inspection, I was shocked at what I saw. I looked at him with a 360-degree view and could immediately see that the entire back of his head was missing. Perhaps he was standing watch and a Yankee sniper simply dropped him where he stood.

On the Earth plane, the body would have dropped and fallen but here - here in this woman's room, he appears as he would have appeared in that half second before his body collapsed. This moment is so instantaneously frozen in that stack of time that the blood has not begun to puddle on the floor, as the lifeblood would have rushed down his body like a red river of instantaneous death. But there is no visible body lying on the ground.

And I found him in Helen's bedroom. He was standing next to her nightstand, by her bed, waiting, not knowing what has happened to him, in an eternal sleep.

A New Definition of Creepy

The Private is standing next to Helen's bed, on 'her side' of the bed. Her husband is sleeping on the other side of her. I have no doubt that if she knew that she had a dead soldier in her room, she would have been chilled to the bone. No one wants a ghost, much less such a young soul who died a lonely and sudden death, to be standing next to you as you sleep, night, after night, after night.

He was specifically standing by the head of her bed, and every night, he unknowingly filled the energy of the room with the essence of his brain death. While he knew no pain in his passing, those around him living in this current time would have eventually become in resonance with him – and with his cause of death.

If you have a ghost living with you, it is possible to become in resonance with this dead person or some facet of them (and in some cases, like cancer, become in resonance with that illness). This aspect could be their emotion at being dead, the kindness or cruelty of their personality, or the pain or injury that he or she would have felt due to their cause of death.

Sandy's chronic series of migraine headaches could be attributed to this dead soldier's head wound. While there is no way to definitively prove this, logic would tell us that if her headaches left after the ghost was removed, that her resonance issue had come to a grateful end. I was anxious to see how she would feel in the coming days and weeks.

The first order of business was to gently awaken the soldier from his not-exactly-eternal sleep. Surprised and bewildered, he thought he had been caught sleeping on watch. Once relieved of his fear, he was grateful to move to the welcoming call of the light.

The Heaven World automatically cares for the wounds of the arriving souls. Pain, illnesses, horrifying injuries that do not receive healing between lives, may leave the newly mortal person with often chronic, undefined pain exacerbated by the inability of almost any medical person to identify it and give it any type of healing. And if the soul does not cross over, he or she never receives this healing. Many times, you have to heal that past life before you can hope to heal the present life.

The Echo of War

The Civil War lasted for five agonizing years. However, the energy ripples of this high-intensity conflict continue to echo out, like the funeral dirge bell that sends its thundering peals into the future, without end. We want it to be over, to close the book, but the energy of war haunts us for a very long time.

Even though you may suspect that you

have the dead of the past on your property, finally learning the truth would still be daunting to absorb. Sandy was grateful to have all of those dead soldiers removed from her land and home; however, she could not fully grasp the concept of how a dead Civil War soldier could have affected her on any level, even though her body was suffering greatly with migraine headaches.

Epilogue

Several weeks later I inquired about her headaches and she was most happy to report that her migraines were or seemed to be a thing of the past and that she did feel better, much better. But she assured me that all of this was because of her new migraine medicine and could not possibly have anything to do with removing a dead Civil War soldier from standing by her bedside who had the back half his head blown away, no . . . nothing at all.

We each find a way to believe what keeps us in that safe emotional place. Ghosts, life in the 4th dimension after death, and being in resonance with the dead, are all obviously extremely challenging concepts. However, what she believes now is irrelevant. The fact that this woman facilitated the removal of thousands of souls is all that ultimately matters.

The Sound of Stomping Feet

Feng Shui Should Have Worked

When you remote view a property, you must always have the homeowner's permission to do anything.

You must work only on the property that the homeowner specifically owns.

You cannot look over to someone else's property to see what ghostly things are happening there – even if you can sense that there is something unusual occurring outside the property line.

So, in the case you are about to read, I am faced with quite a dilemma. My friend Robert is a big proponent of Feng Shui because he has had numerous experiences with ghosts. Robert is the client who was a physician in the Civil War, and I removed over 1000 ghosts from his first home. Eventually, he built a new house in a completely different location and he deliberately filled the interior of his walls with Feng Shui mirrors, facing out to keep the ghosts away from this new property. It was a pretty clever idea and it should have been quite effective.

Imagine my surprise when he calls me and begins complaining that he is hearing this endless pounding. He, and his daughter and his girlfriend all hear it. They are baffled as to the source of this persistent sound. Surely, he tells me, this cannot be a ghost because he as has done all the preemptive things to preclude any more ghosts from coming to his home. Surely the Civil War is over for them.

Surely . . .

"Ma'am, we ain't got no place else to go . . ."

Robert requested that I immediately remote view his property and let him know what could possibly be there, this time.

So, I did. The next night I remote viewed his property. I could clearly see his house and the dozens of Feng Shui mirrors embedded in the insulation in the walls, which were, just as I had anticipated, shining out like spotlights. They provided a powerful force field for the property. Technically, they were exceptionally effective, except for one sticky issue. They were only effective to the very edge of his property line. Neither he nor I had any idea that he would need protection from the dead beyond that.

I have done thousands of remote views and encountered literally millions of fascinating souls.

I have watched as the dead have worked in an astounding array of methodologies to get someone's attention, from moving furniture, and raining inside houses to steadily rocking chairs and terrifying living house pets.

I have listened as ghosts have called out, stormed around, or pounded on walls (including my own walls).

Some desperate souls have even launched stomach-turning stenches to be noticed.

So, this situation was truly an astonishing first: one that in all of the thousands of remote views I have conducted, I had never seen before.

My scan of any property always starts by studying the layout from above, looking down on the view. Then I begin to work through each indoor and outdoor area. What made this situation remarkable was that, looking beyond those blazing Feng Shui mirrors, I could see men standing, but not in any haphazard manner. Just outside this perimeter, with their toes 360 degrees around on his property line were Civil War soldiers. I stopped counting when I got to roughly 1000 men. I have no idea exactly how many were there. I only know that as far as I could see in any direction were Civil War soldiers from both sides of the war, standing on Robert's property line patiently waiting for him to bring in someone to help them to cross over.

But they were not standing there silently. They were all creating a stomping sound. A thousand men were stomping their feet in the 4th dimension. It was an astonishing situation to see. I was absolutely speechless. This explained what Robert and his family heard: the stomping of thousands of feet.

When I asked one of them what they were doing there, a tall, tired, tattered young man in a dirty, bloody Confederate gray uniform politely answered me in an old-fashioned Southern drawl:

"Ma'am, we ain't got no place else to go. Can't you please hep us? We've been waitin' so long. We're cold and tired and we're hungry and hurtin'. Please hep us."

"I'll be glad to help you, but can you tell me why you're all stomping your feet?"

"'Cause, ma'am, we ain't got no other way for him, for Robert, to hear us and we can't get past them shiny lights. He's the one, he's the one we comes to for help 'cause he calls you. We know he hears us. Please, ma'am, help us to go home."

This situation created a bit of a sticky dilemma for me: I can only remote view, can only take action with what I find on the owner's specific property. The interesting aspect of spiritual law when it comes to remote viewing is that you cannot work on anyone else's property unless you have their specific permission and I only had permission to work on Robert's house and yard, nothing else. What was I going to do with literally thousands upon thousands of dead all stomping their feet outside his property line when technically I couldn't touch them, and they couldn't broach the line because the Feng Shui mirrors prevented them from crossing that barrier? And I wasn't able to remove the Feng Shui mirrors to let them cross so I could help them.

I took a moment to scan my situation. Thousands of horribly, mortally wounded men impatiently waiting for help. I could feel that their demands were becoming increasingly intense. I also realized that after I had helped Robert one of the previous times, that somehow the 'word' had gone out that Robert would get these desperate souls assistance, no matter who they were or on what side of the war they were on at death.

This whole situation drove Robert to distraction. He did not want any part of it. He wanted to forget that past life and move on with this life. However, karma never allows anything to be that simple.

I decided that the best way to handle a technically dicey aspect of spiritual law was simply to move out on to the public street in front of his house. This then created a spiritual 'right of way' in which, for humanitarian purposes, I was allowed to help these men. This would not impact the adjacent property owners. This felt like an excellent solution and I immediately began work.

I brought in teams of angels to begin the process of transitioning this tremendous volume of souls. Each angel tenderly wrapped a warm, healing coat around each man's shoulders. It was gratifying to watch as each weary warrior turned a worn, tired, dirty face toward the glorious, kind face of the angel. Each angel immediately radiated out a beam of love and healing to the very core of each man. Then with supreme gentleness, the angels began their journey of escorting each soul into the Heaven World. Wives, mothers and fathers, sisters, and brothers, all welcomed them home. It was an exquisitely gratifying image.

When there are these many men, you only

see a few specific faces, or colors of uniforms, but you do have the sense of the large numbers of souls who are making their way out of the hell in which they have been imprisoned. Men who die in war are seldom able to move forward into the light of heaven because of the heaviness of the volume of violence that precipitated their deaths. I had no idea how many that night were there, waiting and stomping.

Requiring immense concentration to manage the scene and the players in front of you, this process took almost all night to complete. You cannot afford to lose focus in another dimension. It is physically and emotionally exhausting work.

Emotional Haunting

Severe trauma and tragedy do not leave a person at death: some deeply harrowing memories create psychological scars on the soul. Past life emotional trauma can arise from abuse, method of death or an experience so powerful, so terrifying, painfully chronic, or shocking, that it leaves an indelible mark on the personality. Emotional haunting is one of the most prevalent yet not well understood forms of suffering from past memories. Once the person reincarnates, usually from the 4th dimension, those subtle scars are born with them. The individual will (normally) not remember anything about any particular past life. Yet, the energy of that past life ordeal may 'haunt' his or her days. The individual tries to find ways to understand or to heal this 'thing,' this 'emotion' that haunts his or her dreams, and influences life in subtle ways.

Robert's painful connection to the Civil War dogged his days. You can never escape yourself. He continued to attract those Civil War soldiers for years and I found myself helping the dead he attracted, over and over again. Upwards to 100,000 or more Civil War soldiers and civilians were assisted in crossing over thanks to Robert's willingness to ask for help on their behalf. Perhaps the aspect of being able to give them the compassionate assistance in death that he could not give them in that poignantly tragic previous life, will help him to heal.

Epilogue

I called Robert and gave him a detailed account of what had happened. I told him I would also check again the following night to be sure I had assisted all of the men who needed help.

Robert said that when the stomping completely ceased, the house felt the calm of a normal home. He explained that the stomping had been subtle, yet unrelenting. When it was over, he knew they were gone. He and his family were grateful that they were able to help those men cross over and find peace.

Robert was aware that he had a connection to the Civil War, which is why he did not seem particularly surprised to hear about all of those soldiers. Some living souls are magnets for service whether the person thinks he wants that job or not. Such was the case here. Roughly, 860,000 men died in the Civil War. It is hard to imagine how many total souls Robert helped. Perhaps now for whomever we helped, the Civil War can finally be over.

Understanding
Spiritual Science

Throughout this book, you will see different terms applied to moving a ghost into the Heaven World or crossing into the Light of Transition. This is important to understand because, while all ghosts are specifically sent to the Heaven World when they are 'moved on' in these contexts, some are moved to very specific places and that term is called the 'Appropriate Realm.' You will also see this process referred to as crossing the 'Light Bridge,' 'Crossing Over,' 'Moving On,' crossing that 'Bridge to the Light,' 'Crossing into the Light,' embracing the 'Light of the Divine' and moving to the 'Other Side,' or Heaven World.'

Traveling with the Speed of Thought

So many times, ghosts do not know that

they have died. They continue fighting in that battle, baking that bread, or driving down that road as if those precious seconds before that one life-shattering moment are forever frozen in mindless time and eternity.

However, there are those ghosts who are acutely aware that death has come. Many are quite relieved to leave their physical body. Some are grateful that they no longer feel the pain of disease, the limitation of a deformed or crippled body, or the dimensional restriction of blindness or deafness. These are souls who are truly released from the confines of the mortal flesh and rejoice that they have been emancipated from the limitations of time and space.

These are the souls who travel to visit living people with whom they have been connected in mortal life and they travel at the astonishing speed of thought.

When my mother died, I could feel her visit me at 8pm Pacific Standard Time/11pm Eastern Standard Time. She was in a hospice facility in North Carolina. She was not pronounced as actually having died until much later, but I knew that she left her body at that time. I could feel her standing in my kitchen and I could see her joy at being released from her confining, aged, and unresponsive body.

I knew she would visit each of her children,

return to her beloved house in Greensboro, North Carolina and inspect the house she built in Boone, North Carolina. When people who are aware of their death travel through the ether, they are sometimes interested in 'things.' More often than not though, they visit meaningful locations and they visit people: the ones whom they had complicated relationships with, the ones whom they are heartbroken to leave behind.

Some people linger with the living because if he or she was controlling in life, that selfish desire for control will continue in death. If someone is profoundly worried about how a precious one will handle grief, this person will linger, trying to assuage that sense of emotional abandonment. There are a thousand reasons to linger, to want one last taste of mortal life.

You might ask how someone is able to 'travel' to meet these loved ones. The process is actually quite simple. We are all attached to those we love. In The Lightworker's Guide to Healing Grief, there is an important passage that discusses how we are connected to each other and how ghosts can be attached to us.

"It is important that you also understand how profound these attachments are on other levels. The Hawaiian Huna tradition believes that these physical attachments are real. They considered them to be a unique form of energy even though you cannot see them with your physical eyes. Rather like electricity, which you cannot see but know exists; this type of energy comes from your own life force. In the Huna tradition, these attachments are called aka cords.

These aka cords emanate out from your solar plexus—the area just below your breastbone. This is the place where the cord extends out and makes attachments to everyone you have ever met, to every place you have ever been, and to everything you have ever owned. The longer you are attached or connected to something, someone, or someplace, the stronger your aka cord is. Your thoughts also flow along these fine, filament-like energetic cords. This is why when you are connected to someone and that person is thinking about you, you often sense it. This is also why if you have powerful cords attached in a strong love relationship, you often feel it immediately when the person dies. There are many ways to understand how these cords are eventually cut. The more profound the relationship, the thicker are the aka cords of attachment."

This also explains why when someone we love dies suddenly, we may feel doubled over in nausea. Our emotional/spiritual connections are within our solar plexus, not our heart or head area.

We are all connected in life and in death through these amazing aka cords that exist, even though you cannot see them. Ghosts travel with the speed of thought via these energetic links or aka cords. Death does not cease our connection with friends, family members and beloved pets. It is also why it is critically important to help souls to cross over right away. The longer they linger in the 4th dimension the harder it is for them to feel the light and to cross over. Your assistance is a profoundly loving act of compassion.

The Karmic Clock is Ticking

When a ghost is in the 4th dimension, and realizes that he or she has died, and consciously 'haunts' a person or a location, negative karma is incurred. This is because a ghost is interfering with the free will of the living.

My mother-in-law was an amazing personality. Feisty, controlling, opinionated, determined and devoutly dedicated to her Baptist faith. She died at the age of 90, and several years before she died, she boldly informed my husband that she intended to 'haunt' us as a family after she died. I was dumbfounded at this statement.

My husband, however, was not astounded

by her brazen attempt to control from the grave. I suspect on some level, he had expected her to say or do something exactly like this. To his amazing credit, he did not miss a beat and told her right back:

"Oh no you won't! We know exactly how to fix that. Let me assure you, you won't be haunting us or anyone else!"

My husband knew full well that ghosts incur karma when they haunt the living and I think compassionately he wanted to make sure that she did not incur any negative karma by perpetrating any ghostly visits to our home.

As soon as we learned of her passing, I immediately brought in an angel and had her firmly escorted to the other side. She was buried in Arlington National Cemetery with her World War II veteran husband who served 30 years in the Navy. I watched as an angel escorted her to be able to watch her own funeral. I nodded to her, letting her know that I could see her. She was fascinated to see all of her family there and she seemed at peace. She was allowed to linger but a moment and then she was gone. She never haunted us.

I had an encounter with another ghost many years before when I was just learning how to assist the dead. One day when I was driving down the road, to my complete surprise, a very bossy female ghost in a 1960s era yellow Chanel suit jumped in my car. This completely distracted me, causing me to run a red light. I knew it was happening, but I could not get my brakes to work. I bumped into another car, and no one was injured but it could have been much worse. That ghost incurred the karma of causing an accident that interfered with my life and the life of the man whose car I dented. I was eventually able to assist her in crossing over, but she was one angry, controlling woman. She eventually explained how furious she was with her life and why she deliberately drove her car into a tree while extremely drunk, causing her death, some 35 years earlier. I was very glad to see her leave!

Another haunting case involved a controlling ghost who haunted her grown daughter for 10 years before the daughter was able to find help in moving her to the appropriate realm. This vicious mother delighted in tormenting her daughter in life and in death. This ghostly woman caused her daughter to lose sleep because she chattered to her all night, to suffer in relationships because she deliberately drove men away and to feel chronically depressed because of the intense negativity of her mother's haunting presence. The difference the daughter felt, once her extremely narcissistic ghostly mother was no longer able to control her, was liberating. The daughter could now sleep and feel happiness knowing that she was finally alone in her own home and body. That ghost incurred detrimental karma by harassing her living daughter for 10 years.

Another story of ghostly karma involved a young mother's homicidal ghostly father who almost pushed her to the point of murder and suicide. This horrible, ghostly father never ceased demanding that his living daughter murder her four-year-old daughter, and then kill herself. She might have thought she was going crazy but for one chilling reason: her little girl had a habit of repeating what she heard, and she heard her vicious grandfather telling her mother to do these terrible acts. Once that mom and I worked together, and this brutal man was sent to the appropriate realm, the 4-year-old mimic ceased saying those things. This further confirmed to the mother that her father had successfully been removed – finally – from her life. And he incurred horrific karma for doing this to her after he died. Imagine what karma he could have incurred had his daughter actually committed murder and suicide!

It's not just the concept of not crossing over into the light that actually incurs the most intense karma. The issue is the profound impact that the dead have on the living.

Consider the example of the above story of the murderous father: the karma of continuing to try to kill his daughter was horrific.

Even when a ghost 'thinks' he or she is helping their living family members, their influence clearly interferes with that living person's free will and that is the primary issue. You cannot interfere with free will without incurring karma. Put another way, in some cases, it is not the ghost's conscious refusal to cross over that incurs the karma. The negative influence, the fear, the interference the ghost has on a living person, is the primary karmic issue.

Other ghosts incur karma by refusing to cross over when the light comes. Some of them died of terrible diseases and end up 'coincidentally' giving their living relative that same illness. This is an issue of resonance. The living person is in resonance with the person who has just died, more so, if the living person was also the caregiver. The harsh reality is that helping someone through a dying process is extremely challenging, exhausting and depressing. While the caregiving relative may be greatly relieved that his or her loved one is no longer in pain, there is also the process of grieving that person's passing. Grief automatically lowers a person's frequency. The previously existing exhaustion coupled with grief lowers this frequency even further. Now add to this the presence of the ghost who hovers around the home and the person who took such diligent care of them. This ghost can unwittingly put their loved one in resonance with the illness that killed them.

This 'lingering' around the living incurs karma and a greater level of negative karma is created when this soul inadvertently participates in giving their living loved one cancer or other diseases. Here again, the ghost 'thinks' that lingering is helping but in the end this disease resonance situation now goes even beyond interfering with free will. Now the ghost is interfering with the living person's opportunity for a full life. There are tremendous karmic ramifications attached to any of these situations.

One of the primary reasons for assisting a ghost to cross over is that you stop that karmic clock from continuing to 'tick.' At some point, we will all want that karmic stopwatch to cease so that we can finally evaluate the life just lived. This also enables those we leave behind to be at peace.

Sage and White Light

The first tool that most psychics will suggest you use to remove a ghost is white light. The standard phase that many psychics routinely offer, is use sage and white light to get rid of a ghost. They seldom tell you how much sage to use or why you use the sage. Neither do they explain to you how to create this white light, or how long to use it or exactly how it is supposed to remove the dead. But let us take a minute and define white light and then discuss why it will not remove the essence of a dead person.

Bringing Down White Light

This is a spiritual practice in which the person visualizes that a glorious white light is descending from God and magnificently filling the requested space. This space can be a bedroom, a house, a car, anything. Theoretically, this is a great exercise. Most people who know about this do this practice for roughly 1-15 seconds whenever they randomly remember to do it.

To be effective, however, spiritual practice must be done at least once a day and preferably twice a day for several minutes or longer to have any lasting effect on a location. If you do this and other practices for as long as you live, it changes the energy and frequency of your location.

Even then, you will find that it initially takes many months of this dedicated visualization to begin to turn any kind of an energetic corner and make a location free of anything dark. And this cannot be all that you do. You will also have to do a host of other things, but for the moment, our discussion is only about the ironic conundrum of bringing down white light.

It is unrealistic to think that you can bring down white light a couple of times and get rid of a ghost. <u>This will not work.</u>

If, however, you have a daily spiritual practice of bringing down white light and you use other tools, for years, then you probably will not have ghosts come to your home in the first place.

If you purchased a 'new' haunted house, meaning that you just purchased it and it is new to you, then bringing down white light a few times will be ineffective. It will not be powerful enough to shift any energy or to remove a ghost from a location that has been haunted for quite a while.

The bottom line is that simply calling down white light once or twice will not work to remove a ghost.

The Sausage and Ceremonies Herb

If you do any research regarding removing ghosts, the second tool many psychics will tell you to use is sage.

Buy bundles of dried sage.

Smudge sage, they will tell you, meaning that you light one end of the bundle and then allow it to burn a white smoke which is supposed to somehow remove all ghosts, dark intelligences, and negativity in general.

Walk around in a circle three times in every room, they say, with the smudging sage bundle.

Burn sage once a month to keep ghosts away.

I hate to be the one to burst this aromatic bubble, but the truth is this: bundles of sage smell very good and are great for sausage recipes, rituals, and ceremonies but sage will never remove a ghost.

Why Sage Doesn't Do What You Think it Does

Burning sage has absolutely, positively nothing to do with removing ghosts, or keeping ghosts out of your house.

Take the case of a woman with a stubbornly determined ghost who wanted to make this living woman her mother. That's right. This little girl ghost was unable to find her real family, so she selected a living person to be her mom. There was just one little problem: the living woman had a daughter – a very alive daughter. This little ghost girl kept trying to stab the woman's daughter so that she, the ghost, could have the living girl's mom. Bizarre, I know, but these things happen to people. And when it happens to you and your child complains and wakes up with all kinds of stab marks on her body, you have to do something about this potentially murderous ghost.

This desperate mom sought out every psychic she could to locate the correct tools to remove a ghost. You guessed it, she was told to use white light and sage.

She tried the white light but since she was not exactly sure how to do this practice much less how long to do it, this was of questionable value to her and had utterly no effect on her ghost.

Next came the sage: our intrepid mom activated every smoke detector in her house burning so much sage.

But the ghost was still stubbornly standing there completely puzzled as to why the mom was doing something so baffling. The sage had no effect on the ghost whatsoever.

Sage simply cannot transcend time and space. Think about this. You are asking an herb to work in more than one dimension. The fact is that burning sage in this current time will not affect ghosts from any past time period. The reason is that the spiritual frequency of sage is simply not strong enough to affect any negative, profoundly sad, despondent, or violent/evil ghosts. Simply put, sage has no horsepower whatsoever.

Sage has been used for millennia in rituals and ceremonies, for purification and for healing. Sage has also been used to try to remove ghosts, but it never works because the frequency of sage is not powerful enough.

However, very soon, this desperately determined mom was about to enter a whole new magical world of strange and unusual esoteric tools.

My Own Spiritual Service

The Gifts from the Magi

I have always found it puzzling that no one ever questions why the three wise men brought such specific gifts to the Christ Child. Have you ever questioned a priest, pastor or minister and asked this question? Did you ever wonder yourself?

When Christ was born, the three magi brought gifts. Magi (the origin of the word for magician) were, in reality, white magicians. They were far more educated than mere holy men and far more skilled in the more mystical elements of the spiritual world than any wealthy king or lord. These were wise men, men whose wisdom and knowledge were eagerly sought on spiritually esoteric levels. So, it is essential to understand why they brought these specific gifts to the Christ Child.

What did they know that we should know, and can we use this knowledge today?

Gold, Frankincense and Myrrh were these gifts. The resonance of gold has important, mystical qualities because it is so pure. This purity allows gold to hold a higher frequency, and gold is a powerful conductor of all types of energy, so its uses are endless. In addition, it also represented wealth and, any new child, especially one with this profound a spiritual mission, would definitely need wealth. However, it was the other two gifts that were uniquely significant for Christ at that time and for all of us right now.

Frankincense and Myrrh are resins from ancient trees in Yemen, Somalia, Saudi Arabia, Ethiopia, and the Arabian Peninsula. Frankincense and Myrrh at various times were exceptionally valuable and, during the time of Christ, may very well have been on an equal par with gold itself. Both Frankincense and Myrrh can be taken internally as an essential oil as well as used on the body. Both have also been used as curatives for all kinds of physical illnesses and for longevity.

However, the resin of Frankincense (Boswellia or Boswellia sacra) and Myrrh (Commiphora myrrha) has a particularly treasured quality. The spiritual frequency of these two resins is so high, that they have the ability to remove ghosts, lower realm intelligences, (little devils), dark magicians and negative energy in general. And they are not the only resins that can do this.

There are two other resins that remove negativity. These resins are Dragon's Blood (from the Dracaena Palm or Daemonorops, Calamus Rotang or Pterocarpus tree) and Benzoin (styrax balsam), which also come from trees in various countries in the Middle East and Southeast Asia. The Catholic Church has used Dragon's Blood and Benzoin resin for centuries in their churches to cleanse them of negative energies. Outside of the Vatican, in Rome, there are pope shops which carry huge, gorgeous glass jars full of Sangre de Dragone, or Dragon's Blood. Priests specifically burn the pure resins themselves. Most people think that incense is being burned before and during a mass, but the pure resins are what are actually lit inside that swinging brass device called a thurible, clearing the aisles of the darknesses people bring to church. You see the telltale white smoke and that amazing smell that comes up immediately and you know you have the real thing: Dragon's Blood and Benzoin.

Never burn the incense of Frankincense and Myrrh, Dragon's Blood, and Benzoin, and think that it will do the same thing. Incense has no spiritual horsepower; only pure resins can shift the frequency of a large structure, and incense has no spiritual muscle to do the metaphysical heavy lifting of shifting energy other than maybe making you feel good for a few minutes. This is primarily because incense is mixed with all kinds of other things, which can dramatically alter the frequency of the product. Only the pure resins themselves have the spiritual frequency, horsepower, and spiritual resonance to remove anything from the 4th dimension that is haunting, harassing or distressing your home.

It is critical to note that these resins will basically eject ghosts from your house for quite a while. However, these resins will not send ghosts to the Heaven World. Use The Crossing Over Prayer© or the additional prayers in The Crossing Over Book© for that task. The resins remove these lost souls for a period of time and some of them never return because your location frequency may have been raised enough to keep them out.

When you use the resins, and cleanse your house, ghosts have to leave because the frequency of the location has risen to a level that makes it extremely uncomfortable for the ghost to remain. However, if you do not do other things to change, elevate and enhance the frequency of your home, then eventually either the same ghosts or new ones will return.

The bottom line is that you have to change how you are living and increase your frequency. [See my book on this: Karma and Frequency©]

So, using Dragon's Blood, Frankincense, Myrrh and Benzoin resins instead of sage will enable you to preclude the presence of ghosts and/or clean negative energy from your home. Using these precious resins and saying The Crossing Over Prayer© will begin to clear your home of ghosts. However, at some point you will want to ask yourself, why am I attracting ghosts in the first place?

Why Are You Attracting Ghosts?

Once you have cleansed your house with the resins, you will be able to think again because the resin combinations have cleared the toxic mental fog that has surrounded you.

Once the interference in the sleep state has ceased, you can sleep at night.

Once you can begin to analyze your situation, you must come face to face with the critical question: why are you attracting ghosts in the first place?

Analyze what is happening in your life. You may feel magnetic to all kinds of terrible problems because when you connect to the questionable spiritual 'tools' listed below, the dark side always demands payment. This payment may be exacted by causing you to feel tired, have financial problems, feel ill, have all kinds of home problems both in your house and your relationships and possibly make your home vulnerable to ghosts.

What causes someone to become attractive to ghosts, dark energies, and paranormal events? There are a number of reasons:

Ouija Boards

If you are playing with a Ouija Board, do not be surprised when things begin to happen. Ouija is not a game. Ouija is a tool to contact to the other side, and it is an opportunity for dark intelligences to enter your home with your permission. The delicious sense of the scary and fun will soon leave you when you realize that your life is becoming darker and darker. The best advice: never use a Ouija Board. If you do have one of these detestable boards, burn it and then put the ashes in aluminum foil and then toss the foil in the trash.

Tarot and other types of Divination Cards

All Tarot cards by their very nature automatically open up a portal to a dark place. This is because using any form of divination (including the incredibly deceiving angel cards,) means that you are asking an unseen force to help you see the future. The Heaven

World does not engage in telling futures because you have an infinite set of futures. And you have this infinite set because you are a freewill being. Much like the Ouija Board, this payment may be exacted by causing you to feel tired, have financial problems, feel ill, have all kinds of problems both in your house and your relationships and possibly make your home vulnerable to ghosts.

Psychics who 'ask spirit' to guide them have no idea who is actually helping them. Any time you request information from the other side, and you do not do something to 'pay' for it, the other side will ultimately take payment from you in the end. You are asking for information from an unseen being. That being can take your energy and that of your client in future payment through any form of misery, financial difficulty, or physical pain. You will specifically be inviting a dark cloud to invade your entire family. No truly spiritual being engages in telling futures. It violates spiritual law because it creates a potential artificial reality, which influences the free will of another person.

Magic Rituals

There are all kinds of magic books out there that purport to help you acquire a lover, get revenge on a friend or family member, or supposedly enable you to find fame and fortune. Some of them may actually work for a while but since you are taking the energy of your desires from an unseen source, this source will eventually demand its payment and you will have no say so about when, where, or how that being will start sucking your energy from you.

Psychic Ability

Let us say that you are profoundly psychic, and you have a natural ability to see and/or talk to ghosts. You notice that they may follow you around and it feels genuinely uncomfortable when they are with you. You may have either always had this problem or just begun to notice it. At some point you will have to learn how to deal with them. The key feature in this will be to learn how to raise your frequency, so that you can change your life.

Shifting Dark Energy

You may also notice that you are pretty sure you are attracting something, and you may or may not be sure it is a ghost. All you may feel is a dark feeling, a bit more than depression and it may grow. This dark sensibility may create within you a gnawing knowingness that there is 'something' haunting you or something is not quite right. If you have no one to share this with, it can be profoundly lonely.

What could have caused this to happen? There are a host of things that can cause this and they can range from being abused as a child, living with abuse as an adult, focusing on negative things in your life, drugs, alcohol, dabbling in black or gray magic or being associated with people who are negative, angry, violent, and cruel. These types of people have a low frequency and they will reduce your emotional/spiritual frequency. This will need to be raised.

You cannot change your life if you do not decide to change that which surrounds you.

You cannot change anyone else; you can only change yourself.

Ultimately you will need to look at yourself and decide if you will want to change your outlook, your friends and anything negative that is influencing you. This may take some time, but it will be worthwhile in separating you from negative things. If ghosts are primarily surrounding you, then working on raising your frequency will ultimately cause ghosts to leave you alone. If that by itself, does not work, you can also try these tips:

1. Focus on positive prayer.

2. Fill your house with angels by asking for their constant presence.

3. Use The Crossing Over Prayer© and The crossing Over Prayer Book© and ask these angels to remove any and all ghosts to the Heaven World on a continual basis, daily if necessary.

4. Burn Dragon's Blood, Benzoin, Frankincense and Myrrh resins as often as you feel necessary.

5. Fill your house with gorgeous music, such as the glorious works of Mozart, Chopin, Vivaldi, Bach, Schubert, Strauss, and Beethoven. This music will automatically raise your frequency.

6. Use a green light at night in your bedroom and in various places around your home. The frequency of a green light may prevent ghosts from entering your location.

7. Wear the essential oil of Frankincense on your solar plexus (that spot between your breasts, just above your breastbone,) on your wrists and on your third eye (the spot just above your nose on your forehead). This also helps to keep your frequency high.

8. Decide to begin your spiritual path. Perhaps these ghosts are there for a reason and that may simply be to awaken you to your spiritual path.

The point of all of this is to help you to grow, and possibly to help the many ghosts who may be part of your life, to cross over into the Heaven World. You can help them. Asking Angels of Transition with The Crossing Over Prayer© to help this ghost to cross over can be of tremendous service not only to the soul who is waiting for this help, but also for your own spiritual growth.

Despite all this, there have been those occasions when individuals did not know about resins or The Crossing Over Prayer©. These families needed a bit more intervention, which is why I ended up helping them.

The stories in this book have offered you different views of how various souls chose to handle their lives and their deaths. Some personalities will haunt you long after you finish this book.

The stories you have just read are all true, however names, locations and minor details were changed to afford the living families their privacy.

Prayers for Sending Ghosts to the Heaven World

The following prayers are excerpts from The Lightworker's Guide to Healing Grief and are provided to help anyone with difficult death situations.

The Crossing Over Prayer

This prayer will assist any soul to cross into the Heaven World. Once a soul has made this glorious transition from this transitory world of darkness into the glorious light of God, the soul will be restored, physically, emotionally, mentally, and spiritually. This prayer will also work on ghosts whom you may not know. This prayer offers all souls the peace of release into the arms of God.

The Crossing Over Prayer©

Dearest Lord above,
I humbly request that you take
any and all souls, who have found
my divine light of service, into
the Heaven World,
right now.

I ask that an angel wrap each
soul in a blanket of healing light,
right now.

I pray that every single soul
will use the Light Bridge provided
by my angelic team to transition into the
Heaven World,
right now.

I send love and healing to all souls
no matter how they died, no matter
their level of guilt, without any judgment
or prejudice whatsoever,
right now.

May the light of your love, Father,
embrace and keep all of these souls
now and forever.
Amen.

A Prayer for Understanding

This prayer will assist you in seeking answers to the often, unfathomable question of why someone you loved has died. The more you say this prayer the more you open yourself to the insight that can come from God.

A Prayer for Understanding

Dearest Lord,
I most humbly pray that I may understand
the loving ways of perfect order.
I pray that I may understand the
cosmic view.

I pray that I may find meaning in my
pain and hope in my yearning heart
at the transition of my
precious loved one [Name].

Please grant me strength and insight
so that in my healing path,
I may be of service
to others.
Amen.

The Compassion Prayer for Suicide

This prayer offers assistance in healing and understanding. Suicide is so painful for family members left behind. There are endless unanswered questions. Often there is a subtle level of guilt that some friends and family members feel because they are convinced that there is something they could have said or done that would have prevented this event from happening.

However, sometimes, we cannot know the pain and sorrow, anger, and internal turmoil that a person was feeling as they left this world. Sometimes, we are not meant to know these things. Sometimes, all we are left with are the questions for which there is no resolution.

Sometimes, all that we can do is pray to God and ask for assistance in healing the soul who so suddenly left and for healing our own bewildered hearts.

Prayers for Sending Ghosts to the Heaven World

Eventually, it is critical to understand that it is important to provide assistance to the soul so that he or she can find the Light of Transition, and the hope of healing.

This prayer can be read completely, or you can read only the sections that are healing for you in this particular moment.

The Compassion Prayer for Suicide

Heavenly Father,
my precious one has ended his (her) life.
Therefore, I most humbly ask that
your gentle Angels of Transition guide my
beloved one to the Heaven World
right now.

I request that forgiveness be given, Father,
for whatever events or circumstances
led to his (her) decision to leave mortal life. I
ask, Father, that you embrace my dearest one
with the depth of your compassion.

I humbly request, Father, that you provide
healing to fill the dark, angry, or profoundly
sad places of his (her) very soul, with the
powerful restoration of the Light of your
Divine Love.

My heart is aching, Father, with deep despair.
I pray that you will help me to understand His
(her) death with your light of compassion and
without judgment.
I humbly pray, Father, for love and healing for
my entire grieving family.

Prayers for Sending Ghosts to the Heaven World
Please help us to understand and accept this
heartbreaking moment and the days ahead,
with your Divine Grace.

Thank you, Father, for loving
[person's name].
Thank you, Father, for loving me.
Thank you, Father.
Amen.

The Healing Prayer for a Murdered Loved One

This prayer is a difficult one to read if you are facing the death of a murdered loved one. Families facing this type of grief often feel betrayed by God, by the concept that God would allow such a terrible thing to happen to someone they love so dearly. Anger at God is not unusual in these times. Families feel that they are also victims of such a tragic situation. Sometimes, individuals find that they disconnect from anything spiritual including the concept of prayer or of healing in this way.

And yet, there can be no healing without God, without reestablishing that divine connection. Sometimes in the darkness of grief and tragedy, this connection helps each of us to hold on and move through each challenging day of dealing with police, detectives, courts and the often, endless unanswered questions.

346

Prayers for Sending Ghosts to the Heaven World

Assisting the soul to cross over is critical to the soul's ultimate healing. However, letting go of someone who died this way is profoundly difficult. It is normal to want to hold on to the soul. However, releasing the soul to the divine will ultimately help all parties to heal. Souls who are released to the Heaven World, find that the Divine can restore them.

If this entire prayer is simply too difficult to read all at once, then simply read the section that works for you at the time. Each stanza is designed to stand alone.

The Healing Prayer for a Murdered Loved One

Heavenly Father, My precious
[name of person]
has been violently taken from me!
Therefore, I most humbly ask
that your gentle Angels of Transition
immediately wrap my beloved
in a blanket of your healing light and then
guide my them to the Heaven World
right now.

I ask that they receive profound
healing on every level, for the fear, pain, and
trauma he (she) may have suffered as death
came.

I pray that now and always,
you will embrace him (her) with the
restoring Light of your Divine Love.
I am heartbroken that I did not get to say
goodbye.

Please, please tell him how much I love him
now and forever.
He didn't deserve for this to happen.
Please tell him how much I will miss him,
and that I will pray for him every night.

348

Prayers for Sending Ghosts to the Heaven World

Letting go is so hard. But I know I must do
this. I want him to heal in every way.
And I need to heal too. I am so angry!
I am so hurt that this could happen
to someone I love so much!

We are all suffering and do not know how to
heal. Please help us to cope with this
unending pain, and the anger in our hearts.

Please help us to find the strength to fill our
hearts with your Divine Grace,
a bit more as each day goes by.

Above all, please help us to face the difficult
days ahead without him.
Please fill us with the Light of your Divine

Grace, to help us to understand and cope
with this heartbreaking moment.
Thank You, Father,
Amen.

A Prayer for my Beloved Animal

We all love our pets and yet when their light leaves our lives, we are often embarrassed to admit how heartbroken we are. Sometimes, we are made to believe that we should somehow just quickly 'get over' the loss of this creature that graced our lives for such a long time.

Grieve your pet. Pray for your pet. Honor the love you shared.

A Prayer for My Beloved Animal

Heavenly Father,
I most humbly ask that you
guide my sweet [name of animal] to the
Heaven World,
right now.

I ask, Father, that you provide love and
healing to my loyal companion, my most
beloved creature, my precious
[animal's name].

I ask, Father, that this valiant animal be
embraced with the healing
Light of Divine Love.

I send gratitude to you, Father, for the time I
had with this wonderful gift you sent me, this
sweet and loyal creature.

I pray that my beloved animal will know how
much I love her (him) now and forever.

I miss my friend, Father.
Please help me to heal my own aching heart.
Thank you, Father.
Amen.

Ghost Stories from the Ghosts' Point of View

Glossary

Affirmation

An affirmation is a positive statement that we say to ourselves to reinforce our sense of self and to heal some part of us that has been wounded.

Aka Cords

Aka cords emanate out from your solar plexus—the area just below your breastbone. This is the place where the cord extends out and makes attachments to everyone you have ever met, to every place you have ever been, and to everything you have ever owned. The longer you are attached or connected to something, someone, or someplace, the stronger your aka cord is. Your thoughts also flow along these fine, filament-like energetic cords. This is why when you are connected to someone and that person is thinking about you, you often sense it. This is also why if you have powerful cords attached in a strong love relationship, you often feel it immediately when the person dies. There are many ways to understand how these cords are eventually cut. The more profound the relationship, the thicker are the aka cords of attachment.

Angels

Angels are divine beings from the Heaven World who work in the 4th and 5th dimensions to help mortal souls. Human beings are not and can never become angels. Any mortal person can call upon an angel for assistance; this is not imposing on any angel. Angels incur positive karma when they are called upon for assistance by a mortal person.

Angels of Transition

These are specific angels who assist souls to cross over into the Heaven World. Anyone can request their assistance as well.

Appropriate Realm

This is a location that people who commit terrible acts of violence are sent. It is a realm within the Heaven World where the fractured soul can find guidance, soul healing, and methodology for balancing the karma of the violent life previously lived.

Archangel

These are a group of angels who oversee other angels. They are considered significantly more powerful than perhaps the lower ranking angels. All angels are on a path of soul evolution. Archangels are simply at a higher stage of spiritual evolution.

Astral Plane

This is the area of the 4th dimension, the land of no time, space or gravity, the dwelling place of ghosts and other lower realm beings.

Aura, Auric Field

This is the protective bubble, force field, immune system that surrounds the human body. This 'field' can be enhanced or corrupted based on what is happening to a person. The aura can change colors depending on the person's emotional state or condition. Some psychics and psychic children can see auras.

Clearing Resins

Frankincense, Myrrh, Benzoin and

Dragon's Blood are powerful resins from Sumatra and the Middle East. When burned on charcoal disks these resins will clear a tremendous amount of predecessor energy, lower realm intelligences and ghosts. Neither sage bundles nor any type of incense will do this, only these resins.

Dimensional Doorway

We live in the 3rd dimension, a dimension of time and space and gravity. However, in the 4th and 5th dimensions, time, space, and gravity do not exist. The ability for ghosts to move between dimensions is greatly facilitated by a doorway between each dimension as well as the assistance of angels who act as emissaries to facilitate the transition.

Divine

The divine is a connection to God and a location where God can be found. It is the powerful, positive energy of the Heaven World. We all access the divine when we pray, send love and healing, and assist ghosts to transition to the Heaven World.

Divine Beings

These are Intelligences who inhabit the Heaven World and who assist mortals in the 3rd, 4th, and 5th dimensions.

Emotional Haunting

The feeling that a ghost or a location is haunting you because of how you are reacting whenever you are there. This can also be an experience from a past life that haunts you, appearing in your dreams or causing you to focus on a particular subject matter throughout your life.

Ether

This is another term for the 4th dimension, where ghosts among other beings, exist.

Frequency

Negative energy, guilt, grief, depression, drugs, alcohol, and toxic people lower frequency. Hope, love, healing, joy, and delight raise frequency. All positive efforts raise frequency. This concept of frequency or vibration at any given moment may determine your level of health.

Ghosts

These are mortal people who have died and who have not transitioned into the Heaven World. They are now souls inhabiting the 4th dimension.

Healing Blankets

A tool any mortal person can request to assist any ghost. These blankets are infused with the essence of the divine and help raise the frequency of any soul to facilitate transition into the Heaven World.

Heaven World

This is the 5th dimensional dwelling place of God, Jesus, angels, and Divine Intelligences. This is the location a person reaches when he or she crosses into the Heaven World. This location also includes various appropriate realms where even violent souls can receive healing for the extreme fractures in their soul that precipitate terrible violence. They also are provided ways to work through the karma of the life just lived.

Intelligences

These are spiritual beings who can inhabit the lower astral or the Heaven World.

Karma

This is the spiritual law that states that for every single action there is an equal and opposite reaction. What you do comes back to you.

Ley Lines

These are the electromagnetic grid lines that cover the entire planet. These lines are critical because they define the migration routes that animals and insects use. All beings depend on these ley lines to help find their way on Earth. Ghosts are often found in greater quantities along the intersections of some of these types of lines.

Light Bridge

This is the term used to describe the divine pathway, which connects the 4th and 5th dimensions to the Heaven World.

Light of Christ Consciousness

This is 'an energy' of light, which any mortal person can request to help a situation, themselves or a ghost who is lost, alone and afraid. This light facilitates transition into the Heaven World and soul healing, regardless of any person's belief in Christ, their particular religion or lack of religious belief.

Light of Compassion

This is a divine light that has the potential to live in the hearts of mortal people as well as in the essence of angels, Divine Intelligences and God. This light spreads love and care, hope and the promise for redemption, forgiveness, and healing for all souls.

Light Lady

This term primarily refers to the author of this book. This is how ghosts generally refer to the author when they see her in their 4th dimensional realm. She appears especially 'bright' to them, literally full of light, hence the reference to 'light lady.'

Light of Transition

This is a unique form of light that comes to a soul who is ready to transition into the Heaven World. This light is the bridge between the 4th and the 5th dimensions. Additional terms meaning to cross over into the Heaven World include:

Appropriate realm

Heaven World
Light Bridge
Moving on,
Crossing over
Bridge to the light
Crossing into the light
Light of the divine
The other side

Light Work

This is spiritual work that helps others in a loving, gentle, nonjudgmental, and non-prejudicial manner, regardless of that person's religion or belief system.

Light Worker

This is a mortal person who seeks to assist the living and the dead in any karmically correct, spiritual manner possible.

Lower Astral

This is an aspect of the 4th dimension, which is the home of very dark intelligences, lower realm intelligences and spiritual vermin. Some people and religions refer to this as hell.

Lower Realm Intelligences

These are beings who are also referred to as little devils, torturers, dark guys who inhabit the lower astral. These creatures can bring great torment to some ghosts stuck in the 4th dimension. These being can also torture living people during the sleep state.

Metaphysics

This is a two-part word: 'meta' meaning beyond or expanding upon, and 'physics' meaning the study of matter in space and time. Literally, metaphysics is the study of physics beyond what we currently think we know and understand.

Predecessor Energy

This is the energy of past people, structures and events that have existed on a particular piece of land or location. This energy can have a powerful effect on those currently living on that property even if the dwelling is brand new. The following types of energy will make any area especially toxic: violent weather, fire, murder, death by almost any method, war, prison/prison camps, meth labs, assault, abuse, bombing – literally any violent act will have an impact on the land or location. The energy lives in the wood, the minerals of the earth and in any structure(s) on that site.

Psychic

This is a person who has at least one of many spiritual abilities beyond what science can reasonably explain. This person may see and hear ghosts. He or she may see into the future, sense things by holding on to an object or be able to 'know' things not routinely expected.

Psychic Protection

Psychic/spiritual protection can include performing spiritual practices including blessing and prayer and requesting Divine protection. A person can wear specific stones for protection such as black tourmaline, tiger eye, kyanite, howlite, quartz crystal (which is continually cleaned and cleared after each use) and other radionics devices (see below).

Psychometry

Psychometry is the psychic ability to sense the energetic information of a location or an object.

Radionic Devices

These are devices a person can wear

which changes the frequency of their body and is reflected in their auric field, making it stronger. A Radionic device can be a stone, or series of stones, a platonic solid, such as an octahedron, or tetrahedron, sacred shape, such as the Fibonacci spiral, the cross or star.

Reincarnation

This is the concept that we live thousands of lives for experiences. We gain the required experiences, die by some method, get stuck in the 4th dimension, or cross into the light, review those life experiences, choose a set of parents and then we are reborn again. A person can reincarnate from the lower astral which explains the source of violent people.

Remote Viewing

This is the psychic ability of being able to physically be present in one location and project your consciousness to another location anywhere in the world, transcending time and space. Once in that location the remote viewer may be able to scan the energy of an area and determine what is happening in the present and/or what happened in the past.

Resonance

In metaphysical terms, the simplest explanation is that you attract who and what you are. You will attract experiences to you based on who and what situations you are in resonance with at any given time. You attract to yourself others who are like you: The Law of Resonance.

Sage

This fragrant herb is wonderful for ceremonies and sausage. However: sage will never remove a ghost, a Lower Realm Intelligence, clear a space or remove predecessor energy.

Shadow Lands

This is the 4th dimension, the place you may find yourself if you are knocked out of your body and end up in an unconscious state and cannot find your way back to your body.

Shaman

The Shaman for any tribe is the spiritual advisor for the entire tribe. He or she may also be the Medicine Man or Woman, helping the tribe to heal physical and emotional wounds. The term Shaman is one of great respect. Usually, these men and women are very proud, peaceful, and wise.

Soul Frequency

Every soul has a specific frequency that defines him or her at death. The higher the frequency of the soul, the easier it will be for that soul to transition to the Heaven World. However, often the method of death or level of guilt and shame will cause a soul's frequency to be much lower inhibiting their transition to the Heaven World

Spiritual

When we say that someone is spiritual, we assume that this means that they are on a positive path. However, being 'spiritual' does not mean that all 'spiritual people' are doing positive light filled things. Some of the people considered to be the most spiritual can be doing some of the darkest acts.

Spiritual Beings

These are beings who exist in the 4th and 5th dimensions. The higher realms of the 5th dimension of the Heaven World offer us the most positive spiritual beings you can imagine, angels, Counselors of Divine

Wisdom, Divine physicians and so many more. However, the 4th dimension also includes spiritual beings who are black magicians, lower realm intelligences, wraiths, tormentors, and other beings best left undescribed. We would be wise to be circumspect and specific when we refer to 'spiritual beings' because they are *not all the same.*

Spiritual Laws

This is the theme and variation of the energy of karma at work. Each law operates in every dimension. Examples:

For every action, there is an equal and opposite reaction.

You attract to yourself others who are like you: The Law of Resonance.

You attract what you fear the most.

Stacks of Time

All time exists at the same time in a specific stack of time. A 'stack' is a specific window or layer of time where something tremendous happened. The energy of that stack of time will keep vibrating out. To heal the current era of time, you often have to heal the past. When remote viewing a specific location, the psychic must sift through what are called stacks to find the specific stack of time that is currently influencing present events.

The 3rd Dimension

This is the dimension of mortal time and space and gravity. Mortal, living people reside in the 3rd dimension. Gravity anchors people in this dimension so that they can experience life because time and space exist here.

The 4th Dimension

This is the dimension of ghosts where time, space and gravity **do not exist**. People who are ghosts, exist in this dimension. It is an existence because they never change the clothes, they died in. They are not aware of the passage of time, even though hundreds of earth-timed years can go by, and they travel at the speed of thought.

The 5th Dimension

This is the dimension of the Heaven World, God, Jesus, Angels, and Divine Intelligences. We cross into this dimension as we enter the Heaven World. This dimension also has many, diverse aspects and when any soul crosses into this dimension, they are immediately routed to the correct are *based on their frequency and the totality of their life experiences and karma created. So even if a murderer is crossed into the Heaven World, he or she will go to the realm of the 5th dimension commensurate with their karmic ledger.*

Thought Forms

All thoughts are 'things' and these things are forms of energy, even if you cannot see them with your physical eyes. Some thoughts are so powerful that they can physically manifest as semi-visible objects and, in some cases, can manifest as physically visible to anyone. You may see them as orbs, or they may seem to be ghosts, or scary apparitions. Psychics who are well schooled can see them in the 4th dimension. Who creates them? Sometimes white magicians create them, and they can look like shafts of bright light. But the more common type of thought form is the type that is created a black magician and can appear to be something terrifying, either in human or non-human animal-like from. Visualizing salt raining down upon them, readily removes them for they do not have strength in their shape but before you remove them, it can be unnerving the first few times you see them.

Vibration

Please see Frequency.

Wraiths

These are intelligences, energies, and manifestations from the lower realms, from hell. They are dark, evil and can be terrifying. They may appear in a room, a home, or on a piece of property. They are, however, quite fragile and sending them a prayer, or the Light of Christ Consciousness will almost immediately cause them to disappear.

About the Author

Tina Erwin CDR USN (Ret) has studied metaphysics for many years, gaining insight into the interpersonal relationships at the heart of everyday living. Her writing comes from an intense desire to know and understand the unseen world of action and reaction combined with a sincere desire to share this understanding with other knowledge seekers. Her first book, The Lightworker's Guide to Healing Grief© is a treatise on how to help yourself or someone else to heal grief. Her second book, The Lightworker's Guide to Everyday Karma© is a lighthearted look at applying the principles of karmic law to everyday life.

Her next books: Ghost Stories from the Ghost's Point of View Trilogy Volumes 1, 2 and 3© introduced to people what it is like to be dead, what it is like to discover that the life you thought you were going to have is never going to happen. Literally you see the ghosts' point of view.

Soul Evolution, Past Lives and Karmic

Ties© and Karma and Frequency© are both fascinating tools to understanding the more esoteric elements of who we are, why we are here and how we can build better lives.

The Crossing Over Prayer Book© offers the reader 88 amazing prayers to help themselves and others, including the dead. This is an invaluable tool.

Her lifelong studies into the deeper meaning of events and actions were further enhanced by the experiences of a dynamic 20-year career in the Navy, working for the U.S. Submarine Force, retiring at the Commander level. Commander Erwin found the Navy to be a tremendous schoolhouse in which to study all the facets of behavior, from the worst to the finest levels of humanity.

You can learn more about her books, and her videos on her website: www.TinaErwin.com or connect with her at Tina@Tinaerwin.com. You can also reach her at GhostHelpers.com or Contact@GhostHelpers.com

www.ingramcontent.com/pod-product-compliance
Lightning Source LLC
Chambersburg PA
CBHW030909090426
42737CB00007B/136

LESSON PLAN

[ENGLISH]

For

B.Ed., JBT, DIET, PTT, NIT, BSTC, AND OTHERS

Gullybaba.com Amazon.in GPHbook.com

BESTSELLER

Useful For

IGNOU, KSOU (Karnataka), Bihar University (Muzaffarpur), Nalanda University, Jamia Millia Islamia, Vardhman Mahaveer Open University (Kota), Uttarakhand Open University, Kurukshetra University, Himachal Pradesh University, Seva Sadan's College of Education (Maharashtra), Lalit Narayan Mithila University, Andhra University, Pt. Sunderlal Sharma (Open) University (Bilaspur), Annamalai University, Bangalore University, Bharathiar University, Bharathidasan University, Centre for distance and open learning, Kakatiya University (Andhra Pradesh), KOU (Rajasthan), MPBOU (MP), MDU (Haryana), Punjab University, Tamilnadu Open University, Sri Padmavati Mahila Visvavidyalayam (Andhra Pradesh), Sri Venkateswara University (Andhra Pradesh), UCSDE (Kerala), University of Jammu, YCMOU, Rajasthan University, UPRTOU, Kalyani University, Banaras Hindu University (BHU) and all other Indian Universities.

-Hindi Edition Also Available-

Closer to Nature   We use Recycled Paper

GPH BOOK ™

GULLYBABA PUBLISHING HOUSE (P) LTD.

ISO 9001 & ISO 14001 CERTIFIED CO.

Published by:
GullyBaba Publishing House (P) Ltd.

Regd. Office:
2525/193, 1ˢᵗ Floor, Onkar Nagar-A,
Tri Nagar, Delhi-110035
(From Kanhaiya Nagar Metro Station Towards
Old Bus Stand)
Ph. 011-27387998, 27384836, 27385249

Branch Office:
1A/2A, 20, Hari Sadan,
Ansari Road, Daryaganj,
New Delhi-110002
Ph. 011-23289034
011-45794768

E-mail: hello@gullybaba.com, Website: GullyBaba.com

Edition: 2015

Author: Manmeet Kaur
Copyright© with, Publisher
ISBN: 978-93-82688-30-3

FREE HOME DELIVERY of GPH Books

You can get GPH books by VPP/COD/Speed Post/Courier.
You can order books by Email/SMS/WhatsApp/Call.
For more details, visit gullybaba.com/faq-books.html

Note : Selling this book on any online platform like Amazon,
Flipkart, Shopclues, Rediff, etc. without prior written permission
of the publisher is prohibited and hence any sales by the SELLER
will be termed as ILLEGAL SALE of GPH Books which will attract
strict legal action against the offender.